MACAT

An Analysis of

Geert Hofstede's

Culture's Consequences
Comparing Values, Behaviors, Institutes and Organizations across Nations

Katherine M. Erdman

Published by Macat International Ltd
24:13 Coda Centre, 189 Munster Road, London SW6 6AW.

Distributed exclusively by Routledge
2 Park Square, Milton Park, Abingdon, Oxon OX14 4RN
711 Third Avenue, New York, NY 10017, USA

Routledge is an imprint of the Taylor & Francis Group, an informa business

www.macat.com
info@macat.com

Cataloguing in Publication Data
A catalogue record for this book is available from the British Library.
Library of Congress Cataloguing-in-Publication Data is available upon request.
Cover illustration: Etienne Gilfillan

ISBN 978-1-912302-08-6 (hardback)
ISBN 978-1-912127-35-1 (paperback)
ISBN 978-1-912128-33-4 (e-book)

Notice
The information in this book is designed to orientate readers of the work under analysis,
to elucidate and contextualise its key ideas and themes, and to aid in the development
of critical thinking skills. It is not meant to be used, nor should it be used, as a
substitute for original thinking or in place of original writing or research. References and
notes are provided for informational purposes and their presence does not constitute
endorsement of the information or opinions therein. This book is presented solely for
educational purposes. It is sold on the understanding that the publisher is not engaged
to provide any scholarly advice. The publisher has made every effort to ensure that
this book is accurate and up-to-date, but makes no warranties or representations with
regard to the completeness or reliability of the information it contains. The information
and the opinions provided herein are not guaranteed or warranted to produce particular
results and may not be suitable for students of every ability. The publisher shall not be
liable for any loss, damage or disruption arising from any errors or omissions, or from
the use of this book, including, but not limited to, special, incidental, consequential or
other damages caused, or alleged to have been caused, directly or indirectly, by the
information contained within.

CONTENTS

THE MACAT LIBRARY

The Macat Library is a series of unique academic explorations of seminal works in the humanities and social sciences – books and papers that have had a significant and widely recognised impact on their disciplines. It has been created to serve as much more than just a summary of what lies between the covers of a great book. It illuminates and explores the influences on, ideas of, and impact of that book. Our goal is to offer a learning resource that encourages critical thinking and fosters a better, deeper understanding of important ideas.

Each publication is divided into three Sections: Influences, Ideas, and Impact. Each Section has four Modules. These explore every important facet of the work, and the responses to it.

This Section-Module structure makes a Macat Library book easy to use, but it has another important feature. Because each Macat book is written to the same format, it is possible (and encouraged!) to cross-reference multiple Macat books along the same lines of inquiry or research. This allows the reader to open up interesting interdisciplinary pathways.

To further aid your reading, lists of glossary terms and people mentioned are included at the end of this book (these are indicated by an asterisk [*] throughout) – as well as a list of works cited.

Macat has worked with the University of Cambridge to identify the elements of critical thinking and understand the ways in which six different skills combine to enable effective thinking.
Three allow us to fully understand a problem; three more give us the tools to solve it. Together, these six skills make up the **PACIER** model of critical thinking. They are:

ANALYSIS – understanding how an argument is built
EVALUATION – exploring the strengths and weaknesses of an argument
INTERPRETATION – understanding issues of meaning

CREATIVE THINKING – coming up with new ideas and fresh connections
PROBLEM-SOLVING – producing strong solutions
REASONING – creating strong arguments

To find out more, visit **WWW.MACAT.COM.**

CRITICAL THINKING AND *CULTURE'S CONSEQUENCES*

Primary critical thinking skill: INTERPRETATION
Secondary critical thinking skill: REASONING

The Dutch anthropologist Geert Hofstede is recognized as a pioneer in the fields of international management and social psychology – and his work is a perfect example of the ways in which interpretative skills can help solve problems and provide the foundation for strong thinking and understanding both in business and beyond. Hofstede's central achievement was setting up an efficient interpretative framework for understanding the cultural differences between one country and another. Working for the international computing company IBM in the late 1960s, Hofstede noted that such cultural differences had huge consequences for international organizations. Up until then, while many inside and outside of business recognized the importance of these differences, little had been done to define precisely what cultural difference was and in what areas of life it was expressed. Hofstede's insight was that if one could interpret and define the dimensions of cultural difference, it would be possible to measure them and act accordingly.

From a vast survey of IBM's employees in several countries, Hofstede originally defined five dimensions of culture: every society could be rated for each dimension, providing a useful guide to the kinds of cultural differences at play. As ever, good interpretative skills provided the basis for better understanding.

ABOUT THE AUTHOR OF THE ORIGINAL WORK

Geert Hofstede, a Dutchman born in 1928, is seen by many as a pioneer in the fields of international management and the study of cultures. After earning a doctorate in social psychology, Hofstede joined global technologies company IBM in 1965 as a psychologist and researcher. He wanted to understand the cultural differences between the company's employees, and created a far-reaching survey that was distributed throughout IBM. He eventually published the results in 1980 as Culture's Consequences, which became his most famous work.

Hofstede moved on to teach management and anthropology at a number of European institutions, also co-founding the Institute for Research on Intercultural Cooperation (IRIC) in 1980. He retired in 1993.

ABOUT THE AUTHOR OF THE ANALYSIS

Katherine Erdman is a visiting scholar in anthropology and archaeology at the University of Minnesota

ABOUT MACAT

GREAT WORKS FOR CRITICAL THINKING

Macat is focused on making the ideas of the world's great thinkers accessible and comprehensible to everybody, everywhere, in ways that promote the development of enhanced critical thinking skills.

It works with leading academics from the world's top universities to produce new analyses that focus on the ideas and the impact of the most influential works ever written across a wide variety of academic disciplines. Each of the works that sit at the heart of its growing library is an enduring example of great thinking. But by setting them in context – and looking at the influences that shaped their authors, as well as the responses they provoked – Macat encourages readers to look at these classics and game-changers with fresh eyes. Readers learn to think, engage and challenge their ideas, rather than simply accepting them.

'Macat offers an amazing first-of-its-kind tool for interdisciplinary learning and research. Its focus on works that transformed their disciplines and its rigorous approach, drawing on the world's leading experts and educational institutions, opens up a world-class education to anyone.'

Andreas Schleicher
Director for Education and Skills, Organisation for Economic
Co-operation and Development

'Macat is taking on some of the major challenges in university education ... They have drawn together a strong team of active academics who are producing teaching materials that are novel in the breadth of their approach.'

Prof Lord Broers,
former Vice-Chancellor of the University of Cambridge

'The Macat vision is exceptionally exciting. It focuses upon new modes of learning which analyse and explain seminal texts which have profoundly influenced world thinking and so social and economic development. It promotes the kind of critical thinking which is essential for any society and economy. This is the learning of the future.'

Rt Hon Charles Clarke, former UK Secretary of State for Education

'The Macat analyses provide immediate access to the critical conversation surrounding the books that have shaped their respective discipline, which will make them an invaluable resource to all of those, students and teachers, working in the field.'

Professor William Tronzo, University of California at San Diego

WAYS IN TO THE TEXT

KEY POINTS

- Geert Hofstede (b. 1928) is a prominent Dutch scholar known for his work on the values* (ideas of "right" conduct or desirable states of being, fostered over time by structures such as the family or educational system) that form and define a nation's culture.

- *Culture's Consequences*, first published in 1980, uses survey data from the American technology corporation IBM* to analyze the values held by people in more than 70 nations.

- As a study of cultures,* the text is distinctive in its appeal to multiple academic disciplines and in its novel empirical* approach (one that bases its findings on evidence verifiable by observation).

Who Is Geert Hofstede?

Geert Hofstede, the author of *Culture's Consequences: Comparing Values, Behaviors, Institutions, and Organizations across Nations* (1980) was born in the city of Haarlem in the Netherlands in 1928. Experiences in his early life influenced his interest in national cultures*—the system of values and practices that serve to distinguish one nation from another. During World War II,* when Hofstede was an adolescent, the extreme right wing Nazi* Germany invaded and occupied Holland. After the war, he went on trips to Indonesia and England, where he saw cultures that differed from his own. Those early experiences with cultural differences influenced his research interests later in life. At Delft Technical University,* he studied engineering, and he later earned a doctorate in social psychology from Groningen University.*

Hofstede gained practical managerial and industrial experience working for several Dutch corporations. The IBM Corporation, a large multinational company specializing in new technologies, hired Hofstede as a psychologist and researcher in 1965. The corporation had branches in over 70 countries and did business in at least 20 languages.

While at IBM, Hofstede directed a large multinational survey to understand the cultural differences among the company's employees. He strongly supported the study of national cultures arguing that "the survival of mankind will depend to a large extent on the ability of people who think differently to act together."[1] Using the IBM survey data, he identified and studied four "dimensions"* of national cultures.

We can think of these "dimensions of culture" as a conceptual framework that allows us to systematically analyze cultural differences from nation to nation through the identification of polar opposites, such as good and bad, or high and low.

After Hofstede published the results of the study in *Culture's Consequences*, his most famous work, he continued his career as a researcher at several institutions and universities. Many people view him as a pioneer in the fields of cultural studies and international management* (the management of a company or organization that conducts business in more than one country).

What Does *Culture's Consequences* Say?

Culture's Consequences studies national cultural differences through the analysis of empirical data—information verifiable by observation. It was the first such study to use this approach. Between 1967 and 1973, Hofstede collected data from employees at IBM using a survey. He and his colleagues wrote the survey in 20 languages and distributed it to IBM offices in more than 70 countries. The goal of the survey was to gather information to study national values across many nations.

We can define values as the desirable conditions or states of being that a society prefers. They are found at the root of each culture. One way of thinking through a society's values is to imagine a target. If "core values" are the center, the things that express those values can be found in each ring, moving outwards. Closest to the center are the society's rituals* (actions designed to represent its values); the next ring belongs to the society's heroes* (people who represent its core values); the largest ring belongs to the society's symbols* (objects or gestures that have meanings relating to its core values). The rituals, heroes, and symbols of a culture are practice-based and may change over time, but their values are less likely to change.

People first acquire their values at a young age from parents and other family members. Educational systems and structures then foster those values through life. Later generations acquire values from their predecessors and repeat the process. Hofstede defines the process of introducing and maintaining values as mental programming.*

Hofstede saw that it might be possible to measure a society's values by collecting survey data from different nations and identifying patterns in the data, which he called "dimensions." Each of the dimensions allows researchers to measure how much, and in what way, a society values such things by placing it on a scale of opposites—high to low, for example. In his theory, societies may value similar things but to different extents and in different ways.

From the data, Hofstede identified four dimensions: power distance* (the inequality within a society), uncertainty avoidance* (a society's level of comfort with the unknown), the opposition of individualism and collectivism* (the level of independence of societal members), and the opposition of masculinity and femininity* (characteristics associated with one gender or the other). Collaboration on a later research project with the social scientist Michael Harris Bond* revealed a fifth dimension of culture: the opposition of long-term and short-term orientation* (looking to the future or to the present). Hofstede measured dimensions in terms of poles, such as high power distance/low power distance.* Based on the results of the survey data, Hofstede placed nations somewhere between those poles as an indication of the values they hold.

In a similar way, Hofstede studied organizational cultures*—the values that an organization establishes, maintains, and fosters and that different people within it share regardless of nation. He found that these cultures also have dimensions, different from national dimensions. Recalling the levels of culture (values, rituals, heroes, and symbols), he suggested that organizational dimensions reflect the outer levels (rituals, heroes, and symbols). These practices can change over time. In contrast, national dimensions are rooted in the innermost layer of culture (values). Values are the fundamental thoughts and beliefs of a society and are less likely to change.

These observations can be used to manage an organization and change its practices to make a better workplace. However, the values that the employees hold cannot be changed. Instead, information about a nation's values can be used to find solutions to management problems. Companies can change their practices to accommodate the values that their employees hold.

Scholars repeated Hofstede's study by applying his framework to other contexts and found his results to be valid. His theories and paradigm*—or conceptual model and theoretical framework—are still relevant in research today. Researchers in a variety of academic disciplines use his approach to study national cultures.

The work also appeals to practitioners because it has real-world uses. Results from these studies can suggest better ways to manage multinational businesses, and Hofstede's work has been influential in the fields of management and psychology.

Why Does *Culture's Consequences* Matter?

Hofstede offers students and researchers the necessary tools to study national cultures. Understanding cultural differences is important; different peoples are interacting more often in a shrinking world, as businesses continue to expand and more people are studying and traveling abroad. Sometimes this can lead to confusion or unintentional offense.

Within the social sciences, Hofstede's research model and theories have changed how many people study national cultures. Prior to his work, scholars tried to understand the differences among nations by looking at their national character* (the collective characteristics used to identify and typify a particular nation). That approach did not use facts to make claims about societies, but instead made qualitative observations*—information that can be expressed using language such as "tall," "blue," or "clear." Such an approach created stereotypes* about societies—broad ideas about an entire people or culture that are not based on reality.

Hofstede developed a way to observe fact-based differences that exist between nations. Relying on empirical data, his approach has made the study of national cultures more scientific.

Hofstede developed a new methodology for studying cultures that other scholars have replicated* in different contexts—that is, they could follow his approach and compare their data to Hofstede's results. Valid cross-cultural studies are now possible because of his method, and people use them for examining all aspects of human life, including politics, marketing, religion, management, and immigration. Globalization—growing political, cultural, and economic ties across national and continental borders—is affecting cultures very quickly today. Hofstede's approach can help make sense of how these changes are impacting different cultures. We can see how and if a nation's values change or if the changes are more superficial (at the level of rituals, heroes, or symbols).

Hofstede encourages the study of national cultures, believing that this knowledge can be helpful for improving all aspects of human societies.

Culture's Consequences shows that, by studying national cultures, we can understand what is important to people from different nations. Hofstede also demonstrates that this information is useful for managing international businesses. Companies can adjust their practices to make their employees happier and more productive.

The application of this idea to other types of organizations, such as international aid groups or volunteer committees, could be very beneficial, as well. Those interested in working with nonprofit institutions or in social services, for example, could use Hofstede's approach to help their organizations achieve their goals. People working with refugees could use information about national cultures to help them transition and adapt to their new home.

NOTES

1   Geert Hofstede, *Culture's Consequences, Comparing Values, Behaviors, Institutions, and Organizations across Nations* (Thousand Oaks, CA: Sage, 2001), xv

SECTION 1
INFLUENCES

MODULE 1
THE AUTHOR AND THE HISTORICAL CONTEXT

KEY POINTS

- Geert Hofstede collected quantitative survey data* (information that can be measured numerically, such as statistics) from the employees of the American technology company IBM.* He worked in 70 countries and used the data to develop a way to study cultures* (the knowledge and values shared by a people) at a national level.

- Hofstede's childhood experiences during World War II* made him realize that not all nations share the same values.*

- Increasing international collaboration demanded better approaches to understanding different cultures and how to manage within them.

Why Read This Text?

Since its publication in 1980, Geert Hofstede's *Culture's Consequences: Comparing Values, Behaviors, Institutions, and Organizations across Nations* has become a classic text in many fields. It is also one of the most-cited texts in the Social Science Citation Index.*[1] Hofstede's methodological approach and the theories he developed in *Culture's Consequences* have inspired hundreds of replication studies* (those which directly copy a particular method from one study to answer a similar question in another study) across many disciplines. The ability to obtain quantitative data about cultures—frequencies and statistics, for example—has meant that scholars who wanted to observe trends over time or between cultures have standardized and concrete data and facts

> **"** Only in the years after 1945 did I fully realize that for five years we had lived under a system in which everything I held for white was called black and vice versa; this made me more conscious of what were my values. **"**
>
> Geert Hofstede, *Culture's Consequences: Comparing Values, Behaviors, Institutions, and Organizations across Nations*

to support their claims; they have not had to rely on qualitative data* (non-numerical observations) alone.

Culture's Consequences explores the differences that exist between national cultures,* those that serve to define a nation, by examining their values. Values are desired or desirable states or conditions within a society, often evident through the ways that the members of that society think or act. In other words, people in every country have different preferences, and the things they think and do are visible at a national level.[2]

The publication of a second edition of the book in 2001 shows the work's continued popularity within the social sciences. Hofstede almost completely rewrote the original text. It now includes replication studies using his methodology as well as independent validation of what he called his dimensions*—a framework for examining and comparing shared values across different cultures. This means that the research is accurate and relatively up-to-date.

Author's Life

Geert Hofstede was born in 1928 in the city of Haarlem in Holland and he spent much of his early life and career in the Netherlands. From his youth, his middle-class parents encouraged "knowledge and intellectual exercise."[3] He and his family lived under the German occupation of the Netherlands during World War II, and after the war he traveled as a ship's engineer to Indonesia and England.

In 1953, Hofstede graduated with an MSc in mechanical engineering from Delft Technical University,* and he later worked incognito as an industrial worker to see for himself how organizations operated at their base level. For 10 years he worked as an engineer in various Dutch companies while completing his PhD in social psychology (awarded by Groningen University* in 1967).[4] In 1965, Hofstede joined IBM Europe as a psychologist. He founded and managed the personnel research department of IBM Europe, where he conducted the largest multinational research project ever to study national cultures empirically.*

Hofstede taught international management and organizational anthropology* (the study of cultures in organizations) at several institutions across Europe, including the *Institut Européen d'Administration des Affaires* (INSEAD),* where he continued to pursue his managerial research. In the 1980s, he cofounded and became the first director of the Institute for Research on Intercultural Cooperation (IRIC).* He also taught at Maastricht University* until his retirement in 1993. He spent much of the 1990s as an honorary professor at the University of Hong Kong, and he maintains affiliations with several research institutes.[5]

Author's Background

The German occupation of Hofstede's homeland during World War II affected him in several ways. He lived under Nazi* ideology, the extreme right-wing ideology that defined Germany in the war years, largely distinguished by its support for its murderous anti-Semitism (prejudice against Jewish people) and racial hierarchies. These ideas contradicted Hofstede's own values, influenced by his Dutch upbringing, and made him aware of national differences for the first time.

The German occupation of Holland meant that he was unable to travel internationally. His trip to Indonesia shortly after the end of the war was a response to those earlier limitations on his travel opportunities. His next voyage was to England, a country that he expected to be similar to the Netherlands because it was also in Western Europe. His surprise at the many cultural differences between the two countries further stimulated his interest in national cultures.[6]

In an attempt to prevent conflict in Europe following the war, a number of European countries began to focus on integrating economically. The Treaty of Rome,* signed in 1957 by Belgium, France, Germany, Italy, Luxembourg, and the Netherlands, created the European Economic Community (EEC),* which aimed to regulate the prices of goods and remove or standardize international tariffs. Under the Merger Treaty* of 1965, the EEC, European Coal and Steel Community (ECSC), and the European Atomic Energy Community (Euratom) united the participating European countries into a single institutional structure that decades later would lead to the formation of the European Union*—an international union defined by political and economic ties among the majority of European nations. In the following years, this increased international cooperation spread into areas of justice, social organization, agriculture, labor, international politics, and culture across Europe.

From the 1950s to the 1970s, the IBM Corporation continued to expand internationally and to develop new technologies. With new facilities and laboratories in different continents, products ranging from electric typewriters to lasers, and research expanding from office buildings to space exploration, IBM was an international corporation of diverse employees at all levels. In 1968, when Hofstede conducted his first survey at the company, IBM employed 241,974 people and enjoyed net earnings of $871 million.[7]

NOTES

1   Geert Hofstede, *Culture's Consequences: Comparing Values, Behaviors, Institutions, and Organizations Across Nations* (Thousand Oaks, CA: Sage Publications, Inc., 2001), xvii.

2   Hofstede, *Culture's Consequences*, 5.

3   Hofstede, *Culture's Consequences*, 523.

4   "The Hofstede Centre," accessed August 31, 2015, http://www.geerthofstede.com/geert.

5   Hofstede, *Culture's Consequences*, 596.

6   "Culture Does Not Exist," Centre for Intercultural Learning, accessed August 31, 2015, www.international.gc.ca/cil-cai/magazine/v02n03/1–3.aspx?lang=eng.

7   "Chronological History of IBM," IBM Corporation, accessed September 4, 2015, http://www-03.ibm.com/ibm/history/history/history_intro.html.

MODULE 2
ACADEMIC CONTEXT

KEY POINTS

- While Geert Hofstede wrote *Culture's Consequences* to appeal to scholars and students working across several social science disciplines, the text focuses on national cultures* and organizational cultures,* discussed mainly in the fields of anthropology* (the study of human beings and their cultural behavior) and international management* (the management of a company or organization that conducts business in more than one country).

- Anthropologists use many approaches to study and explain cultures; the concept of a national culture developed out of an interest in understanding cultural differences at the national level.

- Geert Hofstede drew on the concepts of values* and dimensions*—roughly, a way to measure and compare cultural values—developed by anthropologists, psychologists (those who study mental behavior and conditions), and sociologists (those who study the history and structures of human society).

The Work in its Context

Geert Hofstede's *Culture's Consequences* developed out of changing ideas regarding dimensions of culture* in the twentieth century.

The field of anthropology looks at all aspects of human cultures—the collective ways of thinking, feeling, and acting in the natural world that are shared and socially maintained by different societies. In the nineteenth century, human societies were evaluated on an evolutionary scale of progress that placed "primitive" societies, such as hunter-

❝ Culture determines the uniqueness of a human group in the same way personality determines the uniqueness of an individual. ❞

Geert Hofstede, *Culture's Consequences: Comparing Values, Behaviors, Institutions, and Organizations across Nations*

gatherers* (those who survive by hunting and collecting food), at the bottom and "civilized" (that is, modern* states defined as self-governing territories with defined borders and a certain degree of economic and social complexity and infrastructure) at the top.

An interest in studying modern states developed out of anthropological and sociological areas of study that overlapped. After the American anthropologist Margaret Mead's* classic text, *Coming of Age in Samoa: A Psychological Study of Primitive Youth for Western Civilisation* (1928), interest in the individual and personality took root, influenced by the field of psychology.[1] In the 1930s and 1940s, anthropology moved from examining small-scale societies* (groups consisting of a few dozen to a few thousand people who are more likely to produce for themselves) to looking at the personality traits shared by people in modern states. Scholars attempted to define national cultures, an area of study that "was preceded by a centuries-old interest in 'national character'*—a notion that a population or part thereof ... possesses collective characteristics."[2]

Similarly, scholars continued to examine dimensions of cultures, either by seeking out similarities shared by all or by examining how cultures were different.

Overview of the Field

National cultures are created by the mental programming* (that is, the ways in which the human mind is shaped) that takes place within a culture. All people may potentially share a universal level of programming, driven by our nature as biological beings. There is also collective programming that some members within the same group share, even though each may have his or her own distinctive individual programming.[3] The collective level is where we observe cultures. We can study values, or things that are important to the collective, in order to describe national cultures because they are replicated and reinforced over time through social organizations and institutions such as families and educational systems.

As globalization increased in the 1930s through to the 1950s, many scholars attempted to study national character (an earlier approach to studying national cultures) to understand how members of the international community might better fit together. For example, the US government commissioned the American anthropologist Ruth Benedict* to study Germany, Japan, and Russia during and after World War II* to understand the psychological make-up of America's enemies.[4] However, by the mid-1950s, interest in the subject began to decline, and problems with the approach became apparent. In some cases, the mental programming and historical influences of cultures were ignored, stereotypes* (that is, unhelpful over-generalizations without a factual basis) were perpetuated, and ethnocentrism* (placing value judgments on other societies) was difficult to overcome.

Academic Influences

The Dutch psychologist Adriaan de Groot* significantly influenced Hofstede's general background and approach to social science research. De Groot wrote a book on social science methodology that later became the justification for Hofstede's "structured approach to human issues." Additionally, the Austrian British philosopher Karl Popper's* "theory of the progress of science through falsification"—a method of arriving at secure scientific conclusions—became a key influence in Hofstede's work.[5]

Hofstede looked for better ways of understanding and addressing national cultures through cultural relativistic* approaches. Cultural relativism is the notion that our biases must be acknowledged if we are to understand cultures through our own perspective; accordingly, the values of the researcher were made clear so that any possible biases could be identified.

Hofstede relied heavily on the theory that cultures express the values that individuals in a society hold. He adapted the American anthropologist Clyde Kluckhohn's* concept of values, described as "a conception ... of the desirable which influences the selection from available modes, means and ends of actions."[6] In other words, values are thoughts and actions that are important to individuals within a society and are reinforced over time to define the group. Hofstede saw this definition as additional to the idea of mental programming—the ways in which these values are reinforced through actions within a society from childhood into adulthood.[7]

One of the main influences on Hofstede's work was the "intersubjective"* approach used by the American sociologist Alex Inkeles* and psychologist Daniel J. Levinson.*[8] By examining and summarizing published studies of cultural systems, they identified three standard analytic issues, or "dimensions of culture"* as Hofstede calls them: "relation to authority; conception of self, including the individual's concepts of masculinity and femininity; [and] primary dilemmas or conflicts and ways of dealing with them, including the control of aggression and the expression versus inhibition of affect."[9] These concepts overlap with four of Hofstede's five dimensions.

Such accounts of values and identification of dimensions within culture formed an important basis for Hofstede's research and provided him with the terminology to explain the results of his study.

NOTES

1   Margaret Mead, *Coming of Age in Samoa: A Psychological Study of Primitive Youth for Western Civilization* (New York: Morrow, 1961).

2   Geert Hofstede, *Culture's Consequences: Comparing Values, Behaviors, Institutions, and Organizations Across Nations* (Thousand Oaks, CA: Sage Publications, Inc., 2001), 13.

3   Hofstede, *Culture's Consequences*, 2.

4   Ruth Benedict, *Patterns of Culture* (Boston: Houghton Mifflin, 1934/1959).

5   Michael H. Hoppe, "An Interview with Geert Hofstede," *The Academy of Management Executive (1993–2005)*, Vol. 18, no. 1 (2004), 76.

6   Clyde Kluckhohn, "Values and Value-Orientations in the Theory of Action: An Exploration in Definition and Classification," in *Toward a General Theory of Action*, ed. Talcott Parsons and Edward Shils (Cambridge, MA: Harvard University Press, 1967), 395.

7   Hofstede, *Culture's Consequences*, 5.

8   Alex Inkeles and Daniel J. Levinson, "National Character: The Study of Modal Personality and Sociocultural Systems," In *Handbook of Social Psychology*, edited by Gardner Lindzey and Elliot Aronson, vol. 4 (New York: McGraw-Hill, 1969).

9   Hofstede, *Culture's Consequences*, 31.

MODULE 3
THE PROBLEM

KEY POINTS

- Anthropologists* (people engaged in research into human cultures) and sociologists* (people engaged in research into the history and structures of societies) questioned if it were possible to study national character* because the available methods for collecting and studying data only provided generalized results.

- Another concern was how one might categorize or define national cultures* while recognizing and respecting the differences between them.

- Geert Hofstede studied the values* of national cultures by developing new methods and analyses that were supported by quantifiable data.

Core Question

When Geert Hofstede began working at the IBM Corporation* in the late 1960s, 20 years before the publication of his text, *Culture's Consequences: Comparing Values, Behaviors, Institutions, and Organizations across Nations*, the term "national character" (the collective characteristics used to identify and typify a particular nation) had already lost favor as a concept in the social sciences. Scholars in the fields of sociology and anthropology argued that whole nations could not be studied. Hofstede later observed, however, that researchers simply lacked the methods to do so.[1] Increasing international economic and political collaboration, not just within IBM, required a new methodology to better understand the values each nation held.

> 66 I believe that the crisis of the national character concept in anthropology in the mid-1950s was due to oversimplified theories that could not be improved for lack of adequate research methods. 99
>
> Geert Hofstede, *Culture's Consequences: Comparing Values, Behaviors, Institutions, and Organizations across Nations*

Hofstede, like many scholars, wanted to know answers to three central questions. Can national cultures be studied accurately, and if so, how? How can the observed differences among cultures be used to organize nations in meaningful ways? Can we actually observe the values that are important to different groups?

Questions about the accuracy of such studies remained. To understand values, one needed to study individuals within a culture* (by which we might understand the ways in which a people express and transmit the values and knowledge they share). That, however, was difficult because it is hard to determine how much the values of one person represent those of the group. Equally difficult, as the Turkish social psychologist Çigdem Kagitçibasi* noted, was the fact that the attitudes and behaviors of one society may not overlap with another.[2] How then, to compare entire nations?

The Participants

Many scholars joined the debate about how to identify and organize cultures. For example, the American anthropologist Edward T. Hall* rejected evolutionary and progress-based approaches to defining cultures. Instead he suggested that cultures could be analyzed according to their methods of communication.[3] He said that two types of cultures existed: high-context (those in which a small number of words, which are not obvious to those outside the group, are used to communicate complex messages within it) and low-context (those in which more words are used to communicate, but in which individual words contain less meaning).

Others, such as the American anthropologists Florence Kluckhohn* and Fred Strodtbeck,* used a multidimensional classification of cultures based on their study of five cultures in the southwestern United States.[4] They divided communities according to where their values fell on a scale:"an evaluation of human nature (evil/mixed/good), the relationship of man to the surrounding natural environment (subjugation/harmony/mastery), the orientation in time (toward past/present/future), the orientation toward activity (being/being in becoming/doing), [and] relationships among people (lineality [that is, hierarchically ordered positions]/collaterality, [that is, group relationships]/individualism)."[5]

The American sociologists Talcott Parsons* and Edward Shils* also developed a multidimensional classification of human action to explain dimensions of cultures,* which included "… affectivity (i.e. need for gratification) versus affective neutrality (i.e. restraint of impulses); self-orientation versus collectivity-orientation; universalism (i.e. applying general standards) versus particularism (taking particular relationships into account); ascription (i.e. judging others by who they are) versus achievement (judging them by what they do) and specificity (i.e. limiting relations to others to specific spheres) versus diffuseness (no prior limitations to nature of relations)."[6]

The Contemporary Debate

According to Hofstede, to advance the study of national culture, the focus had to shift from individual personalities to the analysis of societies as a whole. The problem at the time was a lack of appropriate research tools. Without the ability to collect accurate data at the level of society, many theories of national culture could not be supported.

Some studies possessing data also interpreted it incorrectly and produced ecological fallacies*— that is, errors that occur when data about the nature of individuals is based on statistics collected from the individual's group. Such thinking assumes that all members of a group demonstrate the same characteristics. As a result, group stereotypes* can be created. At their simplest, such assumptions boil down to, "People from this group behave in a certain manner; you are from that group, so you must behave in that matter also."

Additionally reverse ecological fallacies* can occur when individual measurements are applied to the group—a process roughly corresponding to "You behave in this manner and are from this group, therefore, the group must also behave in this manner."[7] Hofstede identifies several studies that committed reverse ecological fallacies in their interpretations, including his own analysis in the first edition of *Culture's Consequences*. While conducting a study with Michael Harris Bond,* Hofstede identified a fifth dimension of culture (long-term versus short-term orientation).* Although because of a reverse ecological fallacy in the original analysis, he did not observe this dimension until later.[8]

Hofstede argued that to avoid producing stereotypes in one's research, information about a population should be seen as scientifically valid only when it is "descriptive and not evaluative (judgmental); it is verifiable from more than one independent source; it applies, if not to all members of the population, at least to a statistical majority; [and] … it indicates those characteristics for which this population differs from others."

Statements not meeting these criteria, which have been commonplace in studies of national character, are unsupported stereotypes produced by ecological fallacies.[9] Such errors can be avoided by basing studies on supported facts—Hofstede's pioneering approach to studying national cultures.

NOTES

1   Geert Hofstede, *Culture's Consequences: Comparing Values, Behaviors, Institutions, and Organizations Across Nations* (Thousand Oaks, CA: Sage Publications, Inc., 2001), 13.

2   Çigdem Kagitçibasi, "Social Norms and Authoritarianism: A Turkish-American Comparison," *Journal of Personality and Social Psychology*, 16, 444–451.

3   Edward T. Hall, *Beyond Culture* (Garden City, NY: Anchor, 1976).

4   Florence Kluckhohn and Fred Strodtbeck, *Variations in Value Orientations* (Westport, CT: Greenwood, 1961), 12.

5   Hofstede, *Culture's Consequences*, 30.

6   Talcott Parsons and Edward Shils, *Toward a General Theory of Action* (Cambridge, MA: Harvard University Press, 1951).

7   Hofstede, *Culture's Consequences*, 16–17.

8   Hofstede, *Culture's Consequences*, 38.

9   Hofstede, *Culture's Consequences*, 14.

MODULE 4
THE AUTHOR'S CONTRIBUTION

KEY POINTS

- Geert Hofstede believes it is possible to study national cultures* (the shared values and knowledge assumed to define a nation) as long as such a study is based on and supported by empirical—verifiable, observable—data.*

- Hofstede's position led to the development of new methodologies that allowed for comparisons of cultures at the national level.

- He applied the American anthropologist Clyde Kluckhohn's concept of values,* along with the American sociologist Alex Inkeles* and psychologist Daniel J. Levinson's* "dimensions,"* to the data gathered from an IBM* survey to create the first study grounded in empirical data.

Author's Aims

In the preface to the first edition of *Culture's Consequences: Comparing Values, Behaviors, Institutions, and Organizations across Nations*, Geert Hofstede stresses the importance that understanding cultural differences can make to improving government policies, social and economic organizations, and the lives of citizens. He wanted his work to be meaningful and relevant for policy makers, scholars, and students in the disciplines of comparative management, anthropology,* economics, political science, sociology, comparative law, history, and social geography* (the study of the environment and the society that occupies it.)[1]

After the revisions to the second edition, Hofstede slightly changed his position on his intended audience, stating: "*Culture's Consequences* is

> **"** I still have the mind of an engineer to the extent that I try to be specific; I try to be clear about what I am saying. For example, the idea of quantifying cultures to some social scientists is horrible. I don't mean that cultures can really be quantified in numbers, but if I dare to say that Culture 'A' has more of something than Culture 'B,' I must also dare to give the number ... this doesn't tell everything there is to tell about culture, but it is a way of indicating that there is a difference and the difference is in this particular direction. **"**
>
> Geert Hofstede, "Culture Does Not Exist"

a scholarly book, written for social scientists, using scientific language," since it focuses on the justification and validation of his data.[2] Instead, he pointed practitioners of international management and students to his popular text, *Cultures and Organizations: Software of the Mind*.[3] The revision of *Culture's Consequences* and the publication of a widely available alternative text supports his aim in the first edition— readership from multiple disciplines and backgrounds.

The second edition of *Culture's Consequences* also emphasizes the external validation of the IBM data. There are more than 400 significant correlations between the scores gathered from the IBM survey and other studies. This proves the validity of Hofstede's approach and analysis. The data support the message presented in both his scholarly and his popular text: culture is multifaceted, and can be broken down into different dimensions in order to understand and classify it.

Approach

Employee morale was an important consideration within the IBM

Corporation from its very foundation. Hofstede and his team developed and distributed surveys across the IBM Corporation between 1967 and 1973 as part of the international employee attitude survey program. They translated these surveys into 20 languages and then verified them through back-translations (translating materials back into their original language) for content and clarity. Managers within IBM distributed the surveys, and the respondents returned them for analysis when completed. Hofstede's team collected and entered around 117,000 responses into the IBM database, which contained information about satisfaction, perception, personal goals and beliefs, and demographic data of IBM's employees.[4]

Hofstede discussed at length the methodological concern of avoiding ethnocentrism,* "an exaggerated tendency to think the characteristics of one's own group or race superior to those of other groups or races."[5] Ethnocentrism, both subtle and obvious, is responsible for inhibiting the advancement of national culture studies, often making them flawed from the start. In *Culture's Consequences*, Hofstede notes that ethnocentrism can be present in all levels of a project from research design (imposing values of one country on a study of another, for example), data collection and analysis (questions written by researchers from only one country, for example), to publication and dissemination of results. ("English-language professional journals usually publish articles following their own implicit research paradigm* and style of communication," for example.)[6] To combat these issues, Hofstede used citizens of other countries and other disciplines in order to bring diverse perspectives to the project.

Shortly after Hofstede and his colleagues gave the first surveys to IBM employees, they saw the importance of the information they were gathering. He set out to present it in a way that would offer broad analyses of national trends focusing "on country differences in answers on questions about employee values."[7] In other words, he wanted to see what mattered most to employees in different countries and to compare those differences.

Contribution in Context

Hofstede's research was a massive undertaking involving 72 countries and 20 languages. At the time, his IBM database contained the largest quantity of multinational survey data ever collected.[8]

When Hofstede was writing, many of the previous studies of culture did not take into account geographic limitations, levels of analysis, or empirical data to support their theories. One of the greatest contributions of *Culture's Consequences* to the field is its use of an empirical study based on quantifiable data (the IBM dataset) that could be used to compare cultures at the national level rather than focusing on the values of individuals within those societies. The study also took account of significant factors such as geography to engage more accurately with the data and to identify possible reasons for visible patterns—thus avoiding reverse ecological fallacies* (errors of analysis that occur when a measurement about individuals is based on statistics collected from the individuals' broader cultural group).

Hofstede's multidisciplinary approach, one drawing on the aims and methods of different academic disciplines and data-supported analyses marked the development of a new method for studying national cultures. In the second edition of *Culture's Consequences*, he provides examples of studies—the "elite alumni from the Salzburg Seminar" survey or the "commercial airline pilots" survey[9]—that used his approach, replicated* his IBM survey, and further validated his results.

NOTES

1   Geert Hofstede, *Culture's Consequences: Comparing Values, Behaviors, Institutions, and Organizations Across Nations* (Thousand Oaks, CA: Sage Publications, Inc., 2001), xv.

2   Hofstede, *Culture's Consequences*, xvii.

3   Geert Hofstede, *Cultures and Organizations: Software of the Mind* (New York: McGraw-Hill, 1991).

4   Hofstede, *Culture's Consequences*, 48.

5   Hofstede, *Culture's Consequences*, 17.

6   Hofstede, *Culture's Consequences*, 19.

7   Hofstede, *Culture's Consequences*, 41.

8   Hofstede, *Culture's Consequences*, 48.

9   Hofstede, *Culture's Consequences*, 91.

SECTION 2
IDEAS

MODULE 5
MAIN IDEAS

KEY POINTS

- Geert Hofstede's primary theme in *Culture's Consequences* is the importance of studying cultures* and defining national cultures.*

- The values* held by national cultures can be defined and understood through the dimensions of culture*—a framework that polarizes a group's shared values (good/bad, high/low, for example) in order to compare it across different cultures.

- Hofstede demonstrates that the five dimensions of culture (power distance,* uncertainty avoidance,* individualism/collectivism,* masculinity/femininity,* and long-term/short-term orientation*) can be used to define national cultures based on values that are developed and reinforced throughout a person's life via "mental programming."*

Key Themes

Geert Hofstede's *Culture's Consequences: Comparing Values, Behaviors, Institutions, and Organizations across Nations* has several key themes. The concept of national cultures and the importance of studying cultures are the core ideas on which he bases everything else in the text. Hofstede argues that studies of national cultures should be scientific—that is, that claims are supported by data. The shortcoming of research into national character* from the early and mid-twentieth century was that it was based on assumptions and unverified stereotypes.*[1] Studies of national cultures, however, are rooted in characteristics that can be defined, measured, and organized, he maintains.

> **❝** The comparison of cultures presupposes that there is something to be compared—that each culture is not so unique that any parallel with another culture is meaningless. **❞**
>
> Geert Hofstede, *Culture's Consequences: Comparing Values, Behaviors, Institutions, and Organizations across Nations*

According to Hofstede, national culture is the manifestation of a country's deeply rooted values: things that are preferred by or desirable to the group. For values to continue, he says, "There must be mechanisms in society that permit the maintenance of stability in cultural patterns across many generations." In other words, societies have developed ways of maintaining and promoting values over time[2]—typically through structures such as the family or educational systems.

Values are maintained through mental programming: the collection of ideas and perspectives "that are developed in the family in early childhood and reinforced in schools and organizations,"[3] Hofstede says. He argues that mental programs are constructs,* or "a product of our imagination, supposed to help our understanding" of reality.[4] We can only see the actions and behaviors that are a result of programming at the universal (biological, inherent to all people), collective (societal, shared by some people), and individual (specific to one person) levels.[5]

Using quantitative data* (information that can be expressed numerically, such as statistics) gathered from the IBM survey,* Hofstede identified four dimensions of culture. He found a fifth during the Chinese Value Survey* in collaboration with the psychologist Michael Harris Bond.* There are "two poles between which the dimension's societal norm is positioned," according to the data.[6] The score, when plotted on a graph, shows the value orientation of any particular population. Multinational corporations can also use this approach for managing their organizational cultures*—that is, the way that the people inside the corporation that share its values and knowledge express those values.

Exploring the Ideas

Imagine cultural systems as layers of an onion. The three outermost layers are practice-based. The first, outer layer is made up of *symbols**— "words, gestures, pictures, and objects that carry often complex meanings" that those within the culture understand.[7] The second layer is *heroes**—individuals possessing characteristics that the people in the society value and who serve as "models of behavior." The third layer consists of *rituals**—non-essential activities that express and continue ideas that are important to the society.

At the center of the onion are *values*, which are the core attitudes and beliefs "shared by major groups in the population" and maintained by structures in the society.[8] Practice-based layers (symbols, heroes, rituals) may change more often than inner values. Hence, national values can be studied because they are less likely to change.

The concept of national cultural dimensions is one of the key ideas of *Culture's Consequences*. The first dimension is *power distance*,* or the level of inequality that exists between people as seen and accepted by those with less power.[9] While power distance can be observed in a variety of situations, both the less and the more powerful generally accept it as a way of maintaining order. Hofstede notes that all societies are unequal, but some are more unequal than others.[10]

The second dimension is *uncertainty avoidance*, or both the degree to which societies will tolerate the unknown and the level of anxiety felt within a society when ambiguous situations arise.[11] For example, countries with a low uncertainty avoidance score are more likely to tolerate diversity, whereas xenophobia* (prejudice against people from other countries) is likely to exist in countries with high uncertainty avoidance.

Individualism versus collectivism, the third dimension, looks at the degree of connectedness among members of a society. In individualist cultures (those that place a high value on the rights of the individual), "ties between individuals are loose: everyone is expected to look after him/herself and her/his immediate family." In collectivist societies, "people from birth onwards are integrated into strong, cohesive in-groups" that look after and have unquestioning loyalty to one another.[12]

Masculinity versus femininity, the fourth dimension, is the importance of emotional roles and social goals specific to genders within a society. This differs greatly across different societies. In masculine cultures, there is a strong emphasis for men, and to a lesser extent, women, to be assertive and focused on material success. In contrast, in feminine cultures "both men and women are supposed to be modest, tender, and concerned with the quality of life."[13]

The final dimension, *long-term versus short-term orientation*, measures where people focus their efforts to gain rewards—either in the future (perseverance and thrift, for example) or in the past and present (tradition and preservation respectively).[14] Nations that score high on long-term orientation are more likely to value resourcefulness and legacies, such as family businesses, whereas those that score low prefer quick results and spending money.

Language and Expression

Hofstede wrote the second edition of *Culture's Consequences* primarily for social scientists. He takes a scientific approach by laying out hypotheses, detailing data-collection methodology and data analyses, presenting the results, and comparing them with other findings to describe trends and develop theories.

For each dimension (chapters 3–7), he first introduces the problems and then describes the country indices using IBM-focused questions. Next, he presents replication studies* of the IBM data (studies repeating the methods used in the original study) and discusses validations.

He follows this with the main discussion, describing "the two poles between which the dimension's societal norm is positioned and the origins and implications of that norm for various spheres of life," as supported by empirical data.[15] He shows each particular nation's exact position between the poles of the dimension. Finally, in the second half of these chapters, he gives an in-depth description of the statistics used and their interpretations. The appendices contain information for replicating the study and the scores from each analysis.

Because Hofstede organizes the information consistently, the text is easy to follow, even if it is rich in statistics. Scientific reasoning is clearly evident in the project; he justifies each statement with supporting data presented directly in the text, and he defines uncommon terms, helping to clarify and support his interpretations.

NOTES

1 Geert Hofstede, *Culture's Consequences: Comparing Values, Behaviors, Institutions, and Organizations Across Nations* (Thousand Oaks, CA: Sage Publications, Inc., 2001), 13.

2 Hofstede, *Culture's Consequences*, 11.

3 Hofstede, *Culture's Consequences*, xix.

4 Hofstede, *Culture's Consequences*, 4.

5 Hofstede, *Culture's Consequences*, 2.

6 Hofstede, *Culture's Consequences*, 84.

7 Hofstede, *Culture's Consequences*, 10.

8 Hofstede, *Culture's Consequences*, 11.

9 Hofstede, *Culture's Consequences*, 98.

10 Hofstede, *Culture's Consequences*, 80.

11 Hofstede, *Culture's Consequences*, 161.

12 Hofstede, *Culture's Consequences*, 225.

13 Hofstede, *Culture's Consequences*, 297.

14 Hofstede, *Culture's Consequences*, 359.

15 Hofstede, *Culture's Consequences*, 84.

MODULE 6
SECONDARY IDEAS

KEY POINTS

- The study of national cultures* should draw on the methods and focus of different academic disciplines. It should also be scientific, using many different methods of data collection to ensure accuracy, as well as statistical analysis of empirical data* to make informed interpretations.
- Hofstede's compilation of quantifiable data* meant that differences between cultures* could be assessed and discussed.
- His use of empirical data revolutionized the way cross-cultural studies were conducted.

Other Ideas

The core argument in Geert Hofstede's* *Culture's Consequences: Comparing Values, Behaviors, Institutions, and Organizations across Nations* is the importance of studying and defining national cultures. But several other themes are evident, too.

The most notable is the emphasis on studying national cultures scientifically. Hofstede believes that people should back up any claims that they make about a culture with concrete facts (data). Otherwise, their assumptions about things such as occupations, religions, or traditions can lead to unhelpful generalizations without a factual basis, or stereotypes.*[1] People should validate—or corroborate—"facts" about national cultures. Such validation can occur through replication studies* (studies that use a similar research method), although the quality of such studies can vary significantly.[2]

> **❝ Organizations are symbolic entities; they function according to implicit models in the minds of their members, and these models are culturally determined. ❞**
>
> Geert Hofstede, *Culture's Consequences: Comparing Values, Behaviors, Institutions, and Organizations across Nations*

The data-collection process and also the quality of the data itself are important in any study, according to Hofstede. To ensure quality data collection, one must adopt a multidisciplinary approach. This encourages not only multiple perspectives but also different levels of analysis. For example, anthropology* looks at the entire landscape of human cultures; sociology studies the groups within the landscape; and psychology looks at the individuals within the group.[3] The data collected must also be checked for quality (sufficient sample size, for example).

In the second edition of the text, Hofstede also discusses organizational cultures.* His findings are the result of a study by the Institute for Research on Intercultural Cooperation, or IRIC*—a research organization interested in cross-organizational culture studies that he co-founded and that sought to identify the similarities and cultural differences among several organizations.[4] He identifies six dimensions of organizational cultures, expressed here as oppositional pairs (and which will be further explained below):

- Process-oriented / results-oriented
- Job-oriented / employee-oriented
- Professional / parochial (that is, provincial)
- Open / closed systems
- Tight / loose control
- Pragmatic / normative ways of dealing with the environment.[5]

Exploring the Ideas

Hofstede argues that using empirical data to study cultures means that other studies can validate the results. For him, "Validity implies reliability: An unreliable test cannot produce scores that meaningfully relate to the outside data." In other words, if others cannot confirm the results of his work using the same methods, something is wrong with the study.[6]

To show how valuable such comparisons can be, Hofstede provides several examples of replication studies—including the "alumni of the Salzburg Seminar survey" produced by Michael H. Hoppe,*[7] a specialist in cross-cultural leadership, and the Values Survey Module conducted by Marieke de Mooij,*[8] an expert on the influence of culture on marketing. The Danish economics and management scholar Mikael Søndergaard* conducted an analysis of 61 replication studies based on Hofstede's work and found that they supported and verified his findings.[9]

Hofstede states that "only differences between the scores from at least two countries can be interpreted and compared to the IBM* database, and this only if the samples are sufficiently large (at least 20–50 per country) and sufficiently matched from country to country (that is, similar in all relevant respects except nationality)." In other words, in order to test the data against other cases, it must be of good quality (a large enough sample size) and comparable (similar things are being measured). Hofstede uses these criteria to ensure that his own analyses are viable and to examine other replication studies.

Overlooked

Compared to Hofstede's dimensions of national cultures, scholars have not paid that much attention to organizational cultural dimensions. The dimensions of organizational cultures, briefly described above, are relatively simple to explain:

- "Process-oriented / results-oriented" compares an emphasis on means (how the job is performed daily) with an emphasis on goals (overcoming challenges, achievement-focused).
- "Job-oriented / employee-oriented" pits organizations that monitor employee performance against those concerned with employee well-being.
- "Professional / parochial" describes whether an employee identifies within an organization by job title or position, or by their unit or boss.
- "Open / closed system" refers to how easy or difficult it is for new members to enter into an organization.
- "Tight / loose control" refers to whether the internal structure of an organization is regimented or unpredictable.
- "Pragmatic / normative" describes whether a work environment is interested in ensuring customer satisfaction (pragmatic) or prefers to emphasize ethics and laws as vital for business (normative).[10]

There is one striking difference between national cultures and organizational cultures. National cultures are based on values,* whereas organizational cultures are based on practices.[11] This has major implications when applied to management and business scenarios, particularly in multinational corporations. Dimensions of organizations are more superficial. They can be learned and unlearned, and thus can be managed through changes in practice. This can lead to a more inclusive atmosphere in the workplace and an improvement in employee morale.[12] The dimensions of national cultures, in contrast, produce facts for management: how to work around or with the values of people within a corporation.

NOTES

1   Geert Hofstede, *Culture's Consequences: Comparing Values, Behaviors, Institutions, and Organizations Across Nations* (Thousand Oaks, CA: Sage Publications, Inc., 2001), 13.

2   Hofstede, *Culture's Consequences*, 67.

3   Hofstede, *Culture's Consequences*, 19.

4   Hofstede, *Culture's Consequences*, 395.

5   Hofstede, *Culture's Consequences*, 397–399.

6   Hofstede, *Culture's Consequences*, 67.

7   Michael H. Hoppe, "A Comparative Study of Country Elites: International Differences in Work-Related Values and Learning and Their Implications for Management Training and Development" (unpublished PhD diss., University of North Carolina at Chapel Hill, 1990).

8   Marieke de Mooij, *Advertising Worldwide: Concepts, Theories and Practice of International, Multinational and Global Advertising*. Englewood Cliffs, NJ: Prentice Hall, 1994.

9   Mikael Søndergaard, "Research Note: Hofstede's Consequences: A Study of Reviews, Citations and Replications," *Organization Studies* 15 (1994).

10 Hofstede, *Culture's Consequences*, 397.

11 Hofstede, *Culture's Consequences*, 373.

12 Hofstede, *Culture's Consequences*, 409.

MODULE 7
ACHIEVEMENT

KEY POINTS

- Geert Hofstede's *Culture's Consequences* was one of the first empirical* studies of culture.* Survey data from more than 70 countries supported Hofstede's theories about "dimensions of culture."*

- Hofstede's rigorous research framework and methodology enabled him to analyze and report significant findings related to data in an international survey that the technology company IBM* conducted of its employees.

- Some of the samples collected during the IBM survey did not offer enough data to make meaningful statements about all of the countries sampled, and due to events at the time, some countries were not available to the survey.

Assessing the Argument

Geert Hofstede's *Culture's Consequences: Comparing Values, Behaviors, Institutions, and Organizations across Nations* set out to explore "the differences in thinking and social action that exist among members of more than 50 modern nations."[1] Hofstede wanted to examine the dimensions of national cultures in a way that would be useful for both scholars and practitioners involved in international management and cross-cultural studies. He identified five dimensions of culture that reflect deeply rooted values* in the countries he examined. He also explored the cultures of organizations and identified six dimensions. National and organizational cultural dimensions provide practical information that can be of use to people struggling to manage multinational corporations.

> ❝ *Culture's Consequences* was timely. The growth of international enterprise in the 1960s and 1970s increased the need to know how to manage effectively in the multicultural cross-border setting that had manifested itself by 1980. ❞
>
> Mikael Søndergaard, *Research Note: Hofstede's Consequences*

Hofstede used empirical data, which he analyzed from a multidisciplinary perspective, offering statistical reasoning for each of his analyses. His results strengthened his claims about the dimensions of culture identified in the IBM dataset—the findings of an international survey of the company's employees. The work resulted in a new paradigm* (conceptual model), which Hofstede describes as "a broad conceptual framework related to fundamental problems of human society, which allows qualitative analysis and quantitative measurement."*[2] His work provided a framework and vocabulary for discussion of cultural differences.

Achievement in Context

Perhaps part of the success of *Culture's Consequences* can be attributed to the circumstances of its publication. The psychologists Walter J. Lonner* and John W. Berry* adopted the book for their *Cross-Cultural Research and Methodology Series*, published by Sage Publications.[3] Like Lonner and Berry, Sara Miller McCune, the publisher's president, saw the significance of the study when Hofstede first submitted it in 1978, and she worked to have the book's message widely communicated.

In 1991, Hofstede published a popular text *Cultures and Organizations: Software of the Mind*, based on the findings in *Culture's Consequences*.[4] The book had a wide distribution and was published in 16 languages. Its accessibility helped introduce new readers to

Hofstede's classic. A second updated edition of *Culture's Consequences* in 2001 reintroduced it to a new generation of scholars whose work shows that its principles are still relevant in research today.[5]

Culture's Consequences emerged at the right time. Companies in the early 1980s were expanding, nations were connecting more with one another, and cultural differences were becoming more apparent. The text was vital for its practical applications in a rapidly changing business and international world.[6]

Hofstede's addition of organizational cultures in chapter 8 of the second edition enhanced the discussion of how to use the concept of dimensions in management scenarios. The discovery that the values of organizational cultures are rooted in practice, rather than in core beliefs as in national cultures, has meant that companies can change policies in different countries to deal with diversity or to improve employee morale.

Finally, the use of empirical research in these areas was a new approach within the social sciences that filled a critical research void. The Danish management scholar Mikael Søndergaard's* review of 61 studies that replicated Hofstede's work shows how widely received this new model has been.[7]

Limitations

The text has some limitations. Hofstede conducted the IBM survey between 1967 and 1973, a turbulent period across much of the world. The fear and mistrust caused by World War II* was still a recent memory for much of Europe. The Cold War* both heightened mistrust and limited communication between communist societies and the rest of the world. Capturing information for many African countries was equally difficult; many countries were in a period of reorganization as they claimed their independence from the European nations that had colonized them. Some of these areas were unavailable for IBM to establish branches or were simply inaccessible for collecting survey data in general. To address these issues, Robert J. House,* a professor at the Wharton School at the University of Pennsylvania, set up the Global Leadership and Organizational Behavior Effectiveness (GLOBE)* world study in the early 1990s. It expanded on Hofstede's work and supplied missing survey data for major parts of the world.[8]

In the second edition of the text, Hofstede himself identified another limitation of the study, noting, "I stated [in chapter 1] that research into values cannot be value-free."[9] The results of *Culture's Consequences* reflect not only the values of IBM's employees, but also those of Hofstede. To make his work more transparent, he includes an appendix detailing his own results from the IBM survey and summarizes his personal value system, which is deeply rooted in his early life experiences. In so doing, he showed an awareness that all researchers bring biases to their work that, even with the best intentions, can never be completely remedied. This is partly why Hofstede talks about ethnocentrism* (the assumption that one's own culture is superior to another's) at length in chapter 1. Our biases are with us right from the development stage of research.

NOTES

1   Geert Hofstede, *Culture's Consequences: Comparing Values, Behaviors, Institutions, and Organizations Across Nations* (Thousand Oaks, CA: Sage Publications, Inc., 2001), xix.

2   Hofstede, *Culture's Consequences*, 461.

3   Hofstede, *Culture's Consequences*, xvii.

4   Geert Hofstede, *Cultures and Organizations: Software of the Mind* (New York: McGraw-Hill, 1991).

5   Michael Minkov, *Cultural Differences in a Globalizing World* (Bingley: Emerald, 2011).

6   Michael H. Hoppe, "An Interview with Geert Hofstede," *The Academy of Management Executive (1993–2005)*, Vol. 18, No. 1 (2004), pp. 75–79.

7   Mikael Søndergaard, "Research Note: Hofstede's Consequences: A Study of Reviews, Citations and Replications," *Organization Studies* 15 (1994).

8 Robert House, Paul Hanges, Mansour Javidan, Peter Dorfman and Vipin Gupta, *Culture, Leadership, and Organizations: The GLOBE Study of 62 Societies* (Thousand Oaks, CA: Sage, 2004).

9 Hofstede, *Culture's Consequences*, 523.

MODULE 8
PLACE IN THE AUTHOR'S WORK

KEY POINTS

- Throughout his career, Geert Hofstede's work has addressed issues of international management and organizational cultures,* crossing disciplinary boundaries to include business management, psychology, and anthropology.*

- Much of Hofstede's later work has built upon theories of dimensions of culture* and his conceptual model of empirical analysis* for studying culture* that he proposed in *Culture's Consequences*.

- *Culture's Consequences* is Hofstede's best-known book. It gave him the status of a pioneer in the field of international management* (the management of corporations and institutions across national borders).

Positioning

Geert Hofstede had already been working in the fields of industry and management before joining IBM Europe.* While conducting employee interviews and survey research for IBM, Hofstede noticed how "people within this one very large organization behaved in very, very different ways and had different ways of thinking, yet collaborated within the same organization."[1] Such observations influenced much of the work that followed the first edition of *Culture's Consequences: Comparing Values, Behaviors, Institutions, and Organizations across Nations* (1980).

Hofstede wrote *Culture's Consequences* for professional social scientists, practitioners, and students, and in the text he focused on the justification of his findings, presenting the data to support it. It inspired

> 66 Looking back on 20 years of consequences of *Culture's Consequences*, I feel like a sorcerer's apprentice; after a slow start the book has become a classic and one of the most cited sources in the entire Social Science Citation Index.* 99
>
> Geert Hofstede, *Culture's Consequences: Comparing Values, Behaviors, Institutions, and Organizations across Nations*

a popular, reader-friendly text titled *Cultures and Organizations: Software of the Mind* (1991), which has been published in 16 languages.[2]

Hofstede completely rewrote the second edition of *Culture's Consequences* (2001) to emphasize the cross-disciplinary nature of the text and to include replication studies* and analyses of dimensions that proved his initial findings. The second edition though still held true to the central message of the first one: that cultures can be studied empirically.[3] Hofstede has repeated this message throughout his career. He presents the study of culture in a multidisciplinary way that appeals to scholars and practitioners in the fields of management, international business, anthropology, psychology, sociology, and more.

Integration

Hofstede has published more than 230 articles, chapters, and books on aspects of culture, management, and international business.[4] His earlier publications focused primarily on aspects of management or the relationship between managers and subordinates. Shortly before and after the publication of *Culture's Consequences*, his work shifted to explore ideas of power, leadership, and hierarchies in organizations.

Much of Hofstede's later work stems from *Culture's Consequences*—a major text that came early in his career and shaped his subsequent interest in the study of cultures. Shortly after the release of the book, his other articles and chapters began to focus on cultures, national cultures,* cultural differences, dimensions of culture, and the exploration of a fifth dimension: the opposition between long and short-term orientation. Some of these texts concentrated on clarifying the meanings of terms or further explaining aspects of *Culture's Consequences*. Many of his later articles combined his knowledge of management, gender, behavior, and culture to offer practical solutions for those working in international settings.

Hofstede's work following the second edition of *Culture's Consequences* continues to build upon his major text through continued debate with his critics about its ideas, exploration of social and cultural values* in different contexts or through different comparisons, and a continued interest in issues of international business and management.

Significance

It was not until nearly a decade after its publication that the impact of *Culture's Consequences* could be seen in the study of social sciences. It became a regularly cited text, establishing Hofstede as a pioneer of research into national cultures and an expert in the field of international management.[5]

He did not foresee the success and reception of his work: "My ideas influenced management theory and practice beyond what I tried for. I never planned or expected things to go this way—it is still a surprise."[6] Some of the book's success can be attributed to good publication, distribution, and readership (its selection for the *Cross-Cultural Research and Methodology Series* from Sage Publishing, for example). The book is meaningful to both academic scholars and practitioners in management and international relations who are seeking to better understand how to integrate and work with multiple cultures.

Hofstede's development of an empirically informed paradigm* (conceptual framework) for studying cultural differences and a theoretical approach for understanding dimensions of culture and organizational cultures has defined *Culture's Consequences* as his intellectual legacy.

NOTES

1   "Culture Does Not Exist," Centre for Intercultural Learning, accessed August 31, 2015, www.international.gc.ca/cil-cai/magazine/v02n03/1–3. aspx?lang=eng.

2   Geert Hofstede, *Culture's Consequences: Comparing Values, Behaviors, Institutions, and Organizations Across Nations* (Thousand Oaks, CA: Sage Publications, Inc., 2001), xxvii; Geert Hofstede, *Cultures and Organizations: Software of the Mind* (New York: McGraw-Hill, 1991).

3   Hofstede, *Culture's Consequences*, xxvii.

4   "The Hofstede Centre," accessed August 31, 2015, http://www. geerthofstede.com/geert.

5   Mikael Søndergaard, "Research Note: Hofstede's Consequences: A Study of Reviews, Citations and Replications," *Organization Studies* 15 (1994).

6   Michael H. Hoppe, "An Interview with Geert Hofstede," *The Academy of Management Executive (1993–2005)*, Vol. 18, no. 1 (2004), pp. 75–79.

SECTION 3
IMPACT

THE FIRST RESPONSES

KEY POINTS

- *Culture's Consequences* was praised for its relevancy (fulfilling a contemporary need), rigor (the quality of the research design), and relative accuracy of its findings (the "dimensions"* he identified were validated by other scholars).

- People have criticized the text for assuming that a small segment of the population is representative of an entire nation; recently, some have also criticized it for the obsolete data on which it depends.

- Hofstede has responded to his critics by stating that a segment of the population is acceptable for analyses and that his results have been validated by other studies. He has also reminded his critics that cultures* are historically embedded and that values* change at a slow rate.

Criticism

The first supporters of Geert Hofstede's *Culture's Consequences: Comparing Values, Behaviors, Institutions, and Organizations across Nations* were the psychologists Walter J. Lonner* and John W. Berry,* who published it as part of a Sage Publication series focused on cross-cultural research and methodology.[1] The series had a wide distribution and readership across disciplines. This boosted the book's popularity.

Another favorable response came a decade later from the Danish management scholar Mikael Søndergaard,* who conducted an analysis of how researchers had engaged with the text. He found that they had frequently cited, reviewed, replicated, and used it as a paradigm.* He

> 66 Does Hofstede 'really' capture what he claims to capture? In other words, does his work reflect 'true' cultural differences? 99
>
> Galit Ailon, *Mirror, Mirror on the Wall*

examined 61 replication studies* and identified at least a few—and in some cases all four—of Hofstede's dimensions in other contexts.[2]

Brendan McSweeney,* a professor of organization studies at the University of London, outlined the main critiques of Hofstede's work, which have primarily concerned his research design and interpretations. McSweeney said that "using a large number of respondents does not of itself guarantee representativeness" and that the sample size for some countries was too small to be meaningful. The pool from which Hofstede drew the sample was also limiting, he said, in that it included only employees of particular occupation categories at IBM.* McSweeney thought it was hard to believe that such a narrow sample of people could represent the values* of an entire nation.[3]

McSweeney also suggested that examining culture* at the national level does not work, partly because cultures can exist beyond national borders and multiple cultures can exist within borders. This is particularly problematic when nations merge because areas with different traditions are not technically part of the same country—as, for example, with the reintegration of Hong Kong into China. Complications also occur when national boarders divide cultural groups—the Kurdish people inhabit southeast Turkey, northern Iraq, and Syria, for instance.[4]

In a more recent critique of *Culture's Consequences*, Galit Ailon,* a scholar of organizational cultures and theory, claims that the book has a political element "that reifies a scheme of global hierarchy." She also says that evidence for ethnocentrism* is apparent in the results because

Hofstede overvalues some results and undervalues others.[5] In particular, she charges him with promoting Western values. Hofstede later reminds her, however, "I have often used my own findings to emphasize that there is no such thing as 'the West.'"[6]

Responses
Hofstede himself has actively engaged in debates with his critics.[7] In the second edition of the text, he responds to several key criticisms of his work:

- To the criticism that surveys are not appropriate for measuring cultural differences, he responds that they should not be the only way; interviews, for example, are also useful for accessing this information.
- To the criticism that branches of one company are not representative of an entire nation, he responds that the differences between national cultures were measured: "Any set of functionally equivalent samples from national populations can supply information about such differences." Further, later independent studies have validated these examples.
- To the criticism that the IBM data are old and therefore obsolete, especially in a rapidly globalizing world, he responds that values are slow to change as they are deeply rooted in tradition; recent studies show that values have not changed in the last 20 years—it is the practices that have changed.
- To the criticism that there are too few dimensions, he responds that more can be added, as long as they are "both conceptually and statistically independent from the five dimensions already defined and should be validated by significant correlations with conceptually related external measures."[8]

In spite of Hofstede's responses, many scholars, such as McSweeney and Ailon, still criticize the text.

Conflict and Consensus

Despite some of *Culture's Consequences* shortcomings, Hofstede's work has continued to be referenced and has gained popularity in many journals—the *Journal of International Business Studies,* for one.[9] Among his critics and followers, the size of his undertaking is widely acknowledged. Both his followers and his critics agree that the work is relevant, rigorous, and relatively accurate.

It is relevant because its publication came at a time when international corporations such as IBM were expanding and businesses needed advice on managing diverse cultural groups and people from different countries. As this is still the case in an increasingly globalized world, Hofstede's work continues to be of use.

The book's rigor stems from its research framework and multidisciplinary approach. This appealed, and continues to appeal, to scholars who have been seeking a more credible method for cross-cultural research.

Accuracy is to some extent a relative question, and in this regard, Hofstede's research has been questioned. Søndergaard's analysis of replication studies, however, has demonstrated the relative accuracy of Hofstede's work.[10]

Hofstede maintains that his model of culture is sound, and he has not acknowledged the presence of errors in his research. He stands by his work.

NOTES

1   Geert Hofstede, *Culture's Consequences: Comparing Values, Behaviors, Institutions, and Organizations Across Nations* (Thousand Oaks, CA: Sage Publications, Inc., 2001), xvii.

2   Mikael Søndergaard, "Research Note: Hofstede's Consequences: A Study of Reviews, Citations and Replications," *Organization Studies* 15 (1994), 447–56.

3   Brendan McSweeney, "Hofstede's Model of National Cultural Differences and their Consequences: A Triumph of Faith—A Failure of Analysis," *Human Relations* 55 (2002), 91.

4   McSweeney, "Hofstede's Model," 91.

5   Galit Ailon, "Mirror, Mirror on the Wall: 'Culture's Consequences' in a Value Test of Its Own Design," *The Academy of Management Review* 33 (2008), 900.

6   Geert Hofstede, "Who Is the Fairest of Them All? Galit Ailon's Mirror," The Academy of Management Review 34 (2009): 571.

7   Geert Hofstede, "A reply and comment on Joginder P. Singh: "Managerial Culture and Work-Related Values in India," *Organization Studies* 11 (1990). Geert Hofstede, "Dimensions Do Not Exist: A Reply to Brendan McSweeney." *Human Relations* 55 (2002). Hofstede, "Who Is the Fairest?"

8   Hofstede, *Culture's Consequences*, 73.

9   P.R. Chandy and Thomas G. E. Williams, "The Impact of Journals and Authors on International Business Research: A Citational Analysis of *JIBS* Articles," *Journal of International Business Studies* 25 (1994).

10 M. L. Jones, "Hofstede—Culturally questionable?," (paper presented at the Oxford Business & Economics Conference, Oxford, UK, June 24–26, 2007).

MODULE 10
THE EVOLVING DEBATE

KEY POINTS

- Studies building upon Hofstede's work have demonstrated that there can be dimensions of culture* beyond those he identified in *Culture's Consequences.*

- Other cross-cultural studies examining cultural differences have replicated his research paradigm,* sometimes referred to as the "Hofstede model," leaving a vast intellectual legacy in the social sciences.

- Current scholars are reviewing and updating the strengths and limitations of the approach that Hofstede used in *Culture's Consequences*, allowing his model to serve as a foundation for national culture* research.

Uses and Problems

When later asked about the significance of his work in *Culture's Consequences: Comparing Values, Behaviors, Institutions, and Organizations across Nations*, Geert Hofstede replied: "What I did, and hadn't realized at the time, was I had introduced a new paradigm." That paradigm was a way of looking at differences between cultures* using empirical data.* Countless researchers, including his critics, have adopted his research framework, which has "become dominant … in the field of culture study."[1]

Hofstede's work has stimulated many studies into the dimensions of culture, particularly in the area of cross-cultural psychology. For example, the Greek American psychologist Harry Triandis* has examined the dimension of individualism / collectivism* in greater depth. This is a dimension of culture that measures the degree of

> 66 The disadvantage of replication and extension studies is that they are caught in the straightjacket of my model and therefore unlikely to make basic new contributions. 99
>
> Geert Hofstede, *Culture's Consequences*

connectedness among members of a society where those members either expect to rely on themselves and their immediate family (individualism) or are connected and unquestioningly loyal to a wider social group. Triandis divided that dimension into "horizontal" and "vertical" individualism,[2] where horizontal orientation represents equality and vertical orientation represents hierarchy. When plotted with individualism orientations, horizontal refers to individuals who want to have equal status but still be distinct; vertical describes individuals who want both special status and distinction. The American psychologist Sandra Bem*[3] has also used the masculinity / femininity* dimension to describe values* at the individual level.

The Bulgarian social anthropologist Michael Minkov* is still investigating Hofstede's dimensions. Using the World Values Survey (a survey measuring values through public opinion polls, which began in Europe and later expanded to include 43 societies across the world), Minkov has added a new dimension to Hofstede's five dimensions. He calls this "indulgence versus restraint."[4] This engagement with, and expansion of, the original dimensions shows the continuation of Hofstede's work still going on today.

Schools of Thought

One of the largest projects inspired by Hofstede's paradigm is the GLOBE* (Global Leadership and Organizational Behavior Effectiveness) study by Robert J. House* and his colleagues.[5]

Organized in 1991, this international research project examined the effects of culture on both leadership and aspects of national and organizational cultures*[6] The project aimed to go beyond the limitations of Hofstede's work while following a similar methodological framework, including the adoption of the five dimensions from *Culture's Consequences*.

Using both qualitative* and quantitative data* (that is, both data that can be analyzed in terms of qualities and data that can be analyzed numerically), the GLOBE study was able to identify nine cultural dimensions including:

- uncertainty avoidance* (the degree to which societies will tolerate the unknown or uncertain situations or states)
- power distance* (the difference in influence or power that exists between those who have power and those who do not)
- institutional collectivism
- in-group collectivism
- gender egalitarianism
- assertiveness
- future orientation
- performance orientation (in which job performance is emphasized)
- humane orientation (in which the well-being of the institution's workforce is emphasized)

These dimensions have sparked debate between Hofstede and GLOBE project members over interpretation of the data and the need to divide some of his established dimensions. As Hofstede notes: "Dimensions should not be reified [made "real"] ... They are constructs,* not directly accessible to observation but inferable from verbal statements and other behaviors," and can be used to predict and measure verbal and non-verbal behavior.[7] In other words, we create these measures to better understand and interpret reality.

In Current Scholarship

From the publication of *Culture's Consequences* in 1980 up to 1999, more than 1,800 articles in a variety of disciplines cited it, according to the *Social Science Citation Index,** and it has inspired countless replicate studies.[8] In the 1990s, scholars conducted four major cross-cultural research projects: first, Michael Minkov's World Values Survey; second, the Survey of Values; third, a project by Peter Smith and his collaborators in 2002 on cultural values and management;[9] and fourth, the GLOBE world survey. Despite criticizing Hofstede's work, much of GLOBE's approach drew upon it. GLOBE was able to replicate Hofstede's study and "extend that study to test hypotheses relevant to relationships among societal-level variables, organizational practices, and leader attributes and behavior."[10]

In many ways the GLOBE study not only picked up where Hofstede's work left off but it also addressed the weaknesses of his original study. For example, the GLOBE study measured femininity directly, whereas in Hofstede's study femininity was measured by a lack of masculinity.* Some scholars, such as the international management scholar Praveen Parboteeah* and his colleagues,[11] viewed this as problematic. Of the nine dimensions that Robert J. House and his colleagues identified, six have their origins in dimensions that Hofstede previously discovered. These are uncertainty avoidance, power distance, institutional collectivism, in-group collectivism, gender egalitarianism, and assertiveness. The first three match Hofstede's own uncertainty avoidance, power distance, and individualism.

While the GLOBE study and Hofstede's study view cultural dimensions differently, the relatedness of the projects is evident: Hofstede's study as the point of origin for national culture studies and GLOBE's work as the continuation of studying and organizing cultural differences.[12]

NOTES

1   "Culture Does Not Exist," Centre for Intercultural Learning, accessed August 31, 2015, www.international.gc.ca/cil-cai/magazine/v02n03/1–3. aspx?lang=eng.

2   Harry Triandis, "The Many Dimensions of Culture," *Academy of Management Executive* 18 (2004).

3   Sandra Bem, "The Measurement of Psychological Androgyny," *Journal of Consulting and Clinical Psychology* 42 (1974).

4   Michael Minkov, *Cultural Differences in a Globalizing World* (Bingley: Emerald, 2011).

5   Robert House, Paul Hanges, Mansour Javidan, Peter Dorfman and Vipin Gupta, *Culture, Leadership, and Organizations: The GLOBE Study of 62 Societies* (Thousand Oaks, CA: Sage, 2004).

6   Mansour Javidan, Robert House, Peter Dorfman, Paul Hanges and Mary Sully de Luque, "Conceptualizing and Measuring Cultures and their Consequences: A Comparative Review of GLOBE's and Hofstede's Approaches," *Journal of International Business Studies* 37 (2006).

7   Geert Hofstede, "What Did GLOBE Really Measure? Researchers' Minds Versus Respondents' Minds," *Journal of International Business Studies* 37 (2006), 894.

8   Geert Hofstede, *Culture's Consequences: Comparing Values, Behaviors, Institutions, and Organizations Across Nations* (Thousand Oaks, CA: Sage Publications, Inc., 2001), 462.

9   Peter B. Smith, Mark F. Peterson, and Shalom E. Schwartz, "Cultural Values, Sources of Guidance, and their Relevance to Managerial Behavior: A 47-nation study," *Journal of Cross-Cultural Psychology* 33, no. 22 (2002): 188–202.

10   Hofstede, "What Did GLOBE Really Measure?" 883.

11   Praveen Parboteeah and John Cullen, "Social Institutions and Work Centrality: Explorations beyond National Culture," *Organization Science* 14 (2003).

12   Xiumei Shi and Jinying Wang, "Interpreting Hofstede Model and GLOBE Model: Which Way to Go for Cross-Cultural Research?" *International Journal of Business Management* 5 (2011).

IMPACT AND INFLUENCE TODAY

KEY POINTS

- *Culture's Consequences* remains a classic for a number of disciplines within the social sciences.

- Critics of Hofstede's work suggest he represents cultures* as static (unchanging) and does not consider individual agency (the power of an individual person to act) or context. They also point to political undertones in *Culture's Consequences.*

- Hofstede remains active in debating with critics and often clarifies his position or refers to other works where he has previously addressed major issues.

Position

A Google Scholar citation search for Geert Hofstede's* *Culture's Consequences: Comparing Values, Behaviors, Institutions, and Organizations across Nations* shows that it has been cited more than 13,000 times in the past five years. The book's methodological framework, which requires empirical data* and allows for correlations with other subsequent studies, is alive and thriving in a variety of disciplines today. A survey of various academic journal articles citing *Culture's Consequences* shows its empirical method and dimensions* have had a widespread impact, reaching such diverse fields as human resource management, computers and communication, sociology, applied psychology, management, marketing, and international business.

Researchers have actively applied Hofstede's framework to recent data to look for new correlations.[1] The management scholar Vas Taras and his collaborators use the individualism dimension for their

> **“** Despite criticism, Hofstedean approaches in particular have proved to be resilient to change, perhaps because a dimensional approach to studying national cultural difference offers a lenient framework that easily absorbs alternative interpretations. **”**
>
> Sierk Ybema and Pál Nyíri, "The Hofstede Factor"

research on acculturation patterns of immigrants in Canada.[2] The communications scholars Jonathan Matusitz and George Musambira look for correlations between dimensions of power distance,* uncertainty avoidance,* and "communication technology indicators," such as cell phones and the development of a nation.[3] The marketing and communications scholars Kendall Goodrich and Marieke de Mooij use the individualism dimension* to examine the effects of verbal or electronic communication—social media, for example—on consumer behavior.[4] The dimensions are used to analyze the main social, political, and economic issues facing contemporary multicultural contexts.

Written for multiple disciplines, the book remains a classic, especially for scholars of international management and social psychology. It is a regular source of criticism helping to foster ongoing debates and new research.*[5] Hofstede himself continues to be viewed as an authority in fields such as international business research[6] and intercultural relations.[7]

Interaction

Most scholars are well aware of, and regularly cite in their debates, the main criticisms of Hofstede's work—such as the inappropriateness of surveys for collecting national data and the contentions that a population does not represent an entire nation and that cultural boundaries can exist beyond national borders.[8] However, Sierk

Ybema and Pál Nyíri, in their critique "The Hofstede Factor: The Consequences of *Culture's Consequences*" in the *Routledge Companion to Cross-Cultural Management* (2015), have posed four new concerns about Hofstede's work: its poor conception of change and conflict, agency, context, and power.

In their first concern, they argue that when "postulated as an unchanging core," Hofstede's dimensions offer little flexibility for culture to deal with conflict and change. That is to say, culture is static.*[9] This concern is particularly apparent when nations split and the new entities appear to be culturally different, such as in the case of the recent split of Sudan.

On agency, they argue against mental programming,* saying that it "marks a disregard for individual agency." In Hofstede's model, they say, members in a society become puppets of that culture and only do what they are programmed to do.

Their third issue concerns the context. The IBM* surveyors did not take into account local, political, or social issues, nor did they discuss the connection of work life versus home life and how that might stimulate different ideas of cultures.

Finally, the social scientists Ybema and Nyíri support Galit Ailon's* claim that Hofstede's work has political undertones. Because Hofstede depicts national cultures as neutral, making scores on the value dimensions equally legitimate, his approach leads to stereotyping.[10] They conclude Hofstede's work "tends to be un-reflexive of its own cultural biases and stereotyping effects on cross-cultural practices."[11]

The Continuing Debate

Hofstede has already countered arguments similar to that first criticism raised by Ybema and Nyíri, writing, "Culture change basic enough to invalidate the country dimension index scores will need either a much longer period—say, 50 to 100 years—or extremely drastic outside events."[12] In other words, we need not fear or reassess the dimensions for some time.

To answer their second criticism, Hofstede refers to the individual level of mental programming, which accounts for personality.[13] Personality allows for agency—in the sense of different behaviors and thinking—within a cultural context.

He has not, however, addressed the valid issue of context that Ybema and Nyíri have raised. The context in which a survey is taken, social issues within the organization, or national politics may have an effect that may not be apparent through the statistical results.

Regarding his political agenda, Hofstede argues that much of his work has actually shown that constructs*—subjective theories or ideas—such as "the West" do not exist.[14] He is aware of his own biases and addresses them in Appendix 8 of *Culture's Consequences*.

Hofstede's research continues to inspire debates. Some of these focus directly on his works; others center more on the implications of his ideas.

NOTES

1 Some examples of journals publishing articles which have cited *Culture's Consequences* within the last five years: *International Journal of Human Resource Management, Journal of Computer-Mediated Communication, Annual Review of Sociology, Journal of Applied Psychology, Academy of Management Review, Journal of Marketing, Journal of International Business Studies*, and more.

2 Vas Taras, Julie Rowney, and Piers Steel, "Work-related acculturation: change in individual work-related cultural values following immigration," *The International Journal of Human Resource Management* 24 (2013).

3 Jonathan Matusitz and George Musambira, "Power Distance, Uncertainty Avoidance, and Technology: Analyzing Hofstede's Dimensions and Human Development Indicators," *Journal of Technology in Human Services* 31 (2013).

4 Kendall Goodrich and Marieke de Mooij, "How 'social' are social media? A cross-cultural comparison of online and offline purchase decision influences," *Journal of Marketing Communications* 20 (2014).

5   Galit Ailon, "Mirror, Mirror on the Wall: 'Culture's Consequences' in a Value Test of Its Own Design," *The Academy of Management Review* 33 (2008).

6   P.R. Chandy and Thomas G. E. Williams, "The Impact of Journals and Authors on International Business Research: A Citational Analysis of *JIBS* Articles," *Journal of International Business Studies* 25 (1994).

7   William B. Hart, "Interdisciplinary influences in the study of intercultural relations: a citation analysis of the International Journal of Intercultural Relations," *International Journal of Intercultural Relations* 23 (1999).

8   Brendan McSweeney, "Hofstede's Model of National Cultural Differences and their Consequences: A Triumph of Faith—A Failure of Analysis," *Human Relations* 55 (2002).

9   Sierk Ybema and Pál Nyíri, "The Hofstede Factor: the Consequences of *Culture's Consequences*," in *The Routledge Companion to Cross-Cultural Management*, ed. by Nigel Holden, Snejina Michailova, and Susanne Tietze (New York: Routledge, 2015), 40.

10   Ailon, "Mirror, Mirror on the Wall," 887.

11   Ybema and Nyíri, "The Hofstede Factor," 41.

12   Hofstede, *Culture's Consequences*, 36.

13   Hofstede, *Culture's Consequences*, 2.

14   Geert Hofstede, "Who Is the Fairest of Them All? Galit Ailon's Mirror," *The Academy of Management Review* 34 (2009), 571.

MODULE 12
WHERE NEXT?

KEY POINTS

- *Culture's Consequences* is a classic in the social sciences and will remain a critical text.
- The framework and theories that Hofstede presented in *Culture's Consequences* are used frequently in scholarly research and will probably continue to be used for some time.
- *Culture's Consequences* was a pioneering text in cross-cultural studies because it introduced the use of quantitative data* into the analysis of cultures.*

Potential

Geert Hofstede's* *Culture's Consequences: Comparing Values, Behaviors, Institutions, and Organizations across Nations* laid the foundation for empirical* studies of cultures. Hofstede regularly offers advice and encouragement for researchers examining dimensions* and differences in national culture.* He suggests that studies should:

- Examine at least 10 cultures;
- "Develop their own survey instruments aimed at the particular populations studied and based on empathy with the respondents' situation;"
- Use both in-depth interviews and participant observation;
- Compare the results with other existing studies.[1]

His suggestions and the models that he lays out in the text serve as valuable guidelines for future researchers.

> **❝** What I think I learned is that understanding the big differences in mindsets between people from different countries helps enormously in interpreting what's going on—and where we can and cannot hope for progress. **❞**
>
> Geert Hofstede, in Michael H. Hoppe, *An Interview with Geert Hofstede*

Some scholars have questioned whether the concept of dimensions will survive increased globalization and new technologies. Hofstede believes that the way in which people interact with technology will continue to display their national culture: "Technological modernization is an important force toward culture change that leads to somewhat similar developments in different societies, but it does not wipe out variety. It may even increase difference, as on the basis of preexisting value systems societies cope with technological modernization in different ways."[2]

For example, he notes that cultures that display high uncertainty avoidance* are less likely to use email for important business transactions and will instead seek a face-to-face confirmation or signature.[3] This means that even in a globalizing world where people are sharing more of the same tools and technology, the ways they interact with or treat new technologies will reflect the values* of their society. This will ensure the continuing use of Hofstede's dimensions for analyses.

Future Directions

Hofstede has amassed a large following during his career. Many of his supporters have conducted replication studies* or have tried to expand his work. He has been collaborating with his son Gert Jan Hofstede, another scholar of organizational culture, for some time. With Paul B. Pedersen, professor emeritus at Syracuse University, they co-authored in 2002 an inquiry into training methods: *Exploring*

Cultures: Exercises, Stories and Synthetic Cultures.

Another critical collaboration in Hofstede's career has been with Michael Harris Bond,* a social psychologist at Hong Kong Polytechnic University. Their work on the Chinese Values Survey opened Hofstede's eyes to the fifth dimension of culture: long-term / short-term orientation. Additionally, Hofstede views Robert McCrae,* a personality psychologist at the National Institute of Aging, as "the main contemporary authority on personality measurement and one of the champions of the 'big five' dimensions of personality."[4]

In an interview with the Center for Intercultural Learning, Hofstede suggests that new research looking at consumer behavior could potentially be useful for finding out about a culture.[5] He suggests that when people have extra money, what they spend it on can tell us about the values of a culture. In *Culture's Consequences*, he presents the results of the Dutch social scientist Marieke de Mooij's* marketing studies that validated all four of the IBM* dimensions using data about European consumers.[6] These include, for example, a demonstrated correlation between uncertainty avoidance and foods and beverages that are viewed as more pure, and a correlation between high individual societies and the ownership of detached houses.[7]

He also states: "I like the applications best, people relating my dimensions to phenomena in societies, such as differences in language structure, in savings rates, in consumer behavior, in corporate governance, in medical practice, and endless other fields."[8] Hofstede also suggests that studies examining connections between culture, sexuality, and religion should be a future—and necessary—area of research.[9]

Summary

Students, scholars in the social sciences, and practitioners of international management will find in *Culture's Consequences* a tested and verified paradigm* for their own research on national cultures.

While commonplace today, Hofstede's introduction of quantitative data and statistics into a traditionally qualitative* and stereotype-ridden* area of study revolutionized the field. In addition to his paradigm, Hofstede's dimensions of culture have practical application today in the fields of international management,* cross-cultural studies, social psychology, and more.

Culture's Consequences remains a classic text because Hofstede wrote it with multiple disciplines in mind; everyone can learn or relate to something within it. While scholars still regularly criticize and debate it, this only helps to foster ongoing developments and new studies on national cultures and their dimensions.[10] Hofstede himself continues to be viewed as an active authority in research fields such as international business research[11] and intercultural relations.[12]

NOTES

1   Geert Hofstede, *Culture's Consequences: Comparing Values, Behaviors, Institutions, and Organizations Across Nations* (Thousand Oaks, CA: Sage Publications, Inc., 2001), 465.

2   Hofstede, *Culture's Consequences*, 34.

3   "Culture Does Not Exist," Centre for Intercultural Learning, accessed August 31, 2015, www.international.gc.ca/cil-cai/magazine/v02n03/1–3. aspx?lang=eng.

4   Michael H. Hoppe, "An Interview with Geert Hofstede," *The Academy of Management Executive (1993–2005)*, Vol. 18, No. 1 (2004), pp. 75–79., 78.

5   "Culture Does Not Exist."

6   Marieke de Mooji, *Global Marketing and Advertising: Understanding Cultural Paradoxes*, (Thousand Oaks, CA: Sage, 1998).

7   Hofstede, *Culture's Consequences*, 170, 241.

8   Michael H. Hoppe, "An Interview with Geert Hofstede," *The Academy of Management Executive (1993–2005)*, Vol. 18, No. 1 (2004): pp. 75–79..

9   Hoppe, "An Interview with Geert Hofstede," 76.

10 Galit Ailon, "Mirror, Mirror on the Wall: 'Culture's Consequences' in a Value Test of Its Own Design," *The Academy of Management Review* 33 (2008).

11 P.R. Chandy and Thomas G. E. Williams, "The Impact of Journals and Authors on International Business Research: A Citational Analysis of *JIBS* Articles," *Journal of International Business Studies* 25 (1994).

12 William B. Hart, "Interdisciplinary influences in the study of intercultural relations: a citation analysis of the International Journal of Intercultural Relations," *International Journal of Intercultural Relations* 23 (1999).

GLOSSARY

GLOSSARY OF TERMS

Anthropology: a discipline that inquires into the complexities of past and present humans. It considers aspects of their cultures, such as division of labor, government, religion, subsistence, and technology.

Chinese Value Survey: a study that the social scientist Michael Harris Bond conceived in the early 1980s that asked Chinese colleagues to produce a questionnaire reflecting Chinese (instead of Western) values. People around the world took the survey, and the results identified another dimension of culture.

Cold War: a period from 1947 to 1991 of political, military, and social tension between the Eastern bloc (the Soviet Union and its allies) and the Western bloc (Western Europe and the United States, and their allies) that developed after World War II.

Construct: a theory or idea that is subjective rather than based on facts or empirical evidence.

Cultural relativism: the notion that we have biases that we must acknowledge in order for us to understand cultures through our own perspective.

Culture: the knowledge and values shared by a group of people and socially transmitted over time as a way to make sense of and express the human experience.

Delft Technical University: one of the largest and oldest public technical universities in the Netherlands; located in Delft, it specializes in research and industry.

Dimensions of culture: a framework for studying and understanding cross-cultural comparisons that examines the shared values of a group in polarized form—for example, good/bad or high/low.

Ecological fallacy: an error that can occur when a measurement about individuals is based on statistics collected from the individuals' broader cultural group.

Empirical data: information that is gathered through observation and experimentation.

Ethnocentrism: a way of thinking that one's own culture is superior to another's; making value judgments about a different culture.

European Economic Community (EEC): a regional organization formed in Europe following World War II to promote peace among nations through economic stability, reinforced by such measures as regulated tariffs and prices.

European Union: a union of multiple European countries that have political and social ties, some of whom are united economically under the Euro.

GLOBE (Global Leadership and Organizational Behavior Effectiveness) survey: a study developed by the leadership scholar Robert J. House and his colleagues in the early 1990s to expand on Hofstede's work by gathering survey data from major parts of the world that were not previously studied.

Groningen University: one of the oldest and largest universities in the Netherlands; located in the city of Groningen, it offers diverse educational programs.

Heroes: figures—either alive or dead, or real or fictional—possessing characteristics that are highly prized by a culture.

Hunter-gatherers: a subsistence pattern often characteristic of small groups where both men and women contribute to food procurement by hunting game or harvesting wild vegetation.

IBM (International Business Machines) Corporation: a New York-based multinational and multibillion dollar technology company that is responsible for major developments in the twentieth century, such as lasers, computers, and software used by NASA. IBM Europe is the European branch of the company.

Individualism versus collectivism: a dimension of culture that measures the degree of connectedness among members of a society. They either expect to rely on themselves and their immediate family (individualism) or are connected and unquestioningly loyal to a wider social group.

INSEAD (Institut Européen d'Administration des Affaires): an international business school in Fontainebleau, France, where Hofstede taught management courses.

International management: the management of a company or organization that conducts business in more than one country.

Intersubjective: a term used in psychology to describe when something is accessible between two separate minds.

IRIC (Institute for Research on Intercultural Cooperation): a research organization interested in cross-organizational culture studies that Geert Hofstede co-founded in the 1980s.

Long-term versus short-term orientation: a dimension of culture that measures where people focus their efforts for rewards, either looking to the future (long-term) or the past and present (short-term).

Maastricht University: one of the youngest universities in the Netherlands; located in Maastricht, it offers traditional programs and a liberal arts education.

Masculinity versus femininity: a dimension of culture that measures the importance of emotional roles and social goals specific to genders within a society—with masculine societies more focused on success and assertiveness and feminine societies more focused on quality of life and tenderness.

Mental programming/programs/software: the development or programmed way of thinking that people acquire throughout their lives by exposure to structures or institutions, such as the family or educational systems. The universal level of programming is based in biology and shared by all people, the collective level is based in cultures and shared by some, and the individual level is based in one person's experiences and unique to only that person.

Merger Treaty, or Brussels Treaty: an agreement among multiple western European countries, signed in 1965 and taking effect in 1967, that combined the European Coal and Steel Community (ECSC), European Atomic Energy Community (Euratom), and the European Economic Community (EEC) into a single institution. It can be seen as the beginning of the European Union.

Modern state: a recognized, self-governing territory with defined borders and a certain degree of economic and social complexity and infrastructure.

National character: the collective characteristics used to identify and typify a particular nation, but often the result of unverified facts that can produce stereotypes.

National culture: the values established, maintained, and fostered by citizens and institutional structures within a nation, such as the family or educational systems, that are different from other nations.

Nazism: a branch of fascism created by the Nazi Party (1920–1945), founded on far-right politics, racial hierarchies, and murderously anti-Semitic beliefs.

Organizational cultures: the values established, maintained, and fostered by an organization that are shared by different people within the organization regardless of their nationality.

Paradigm: a theoretical framework containing ideas, ways of thinking, laws, and methodology that is accepted by other scientists and researchers.

Power distance: a dimension of culture that measures the difference in influence or power that exists between those who have power and those who do not, as seen by the less powerful of the two.

Qualitative data: categorical information that can be expressed using language ("tall," "blue," "clear," for example).

Quantitative data: information about quantities that can be measured and expressed numerically; examples might be "25 percent," "3.14," or "5 out of 6".

Replication study: a research study that follows the framework or methods of a previous study but uses new subjects or contexts.

Reverse ecological fallacy: an error that can occur when measurements about an individual are applied to the group.

Rituals: performed actions that are not meant to accomplish anything but are socially important to society; they are performed for their own sake.

Small-scale societies: a small territory or small groups consisting of a few dozen to a few thousand people who are more likely to produce for themselves.

Social geography: the study of the environment and the society that occupies it.

Social Science Citation Index: an index containing citation information for social scientists to use for research and analysis.

Stereotype: a belief about a person or a group of people that is not based on facts.

Symbols: objects or actions that are given meaning by a culture.

Treaty of Rome: an agreement among multiple western European countries, signed in 1957 and taking effect in 1958, that established the European Economic Community (EEC), an economic organization designed to create a common goods market and regulate fees.

Uncertainty avoidance: a dimension of culture that measures the degree to which societies will tolerate the unknown or uncertain situations or states.

Values: preferred or desirable conditions or states of being that a group of people share, and that institutional structures like the family or educational systems foster over time.

World War II: a conflict fought from 1939 to 1945 that involved virtually every major country on earth. Fought between the Allies (the United States, Britain, France, the Soviet Union and others), and the Axis powers (Germany, Italy and Japan, along with their allies), it was seen as a major moral struggle between freedom and tyranny and included seminal events such as the Holocaust.

Xenophobia: the fear or dislike of strangers from other countries; it can be associated with racism or stereotyping.

PEOPLE MENTIONED IN THE TEXT

Galit Ailon is a professor in the department of sociology and anthropology at Bar-Ilan University in Israel. She examines organizational cultures, financial cultures, and organizational theory.

Ruth Benedict (1887–1948) was an American cultural anthropologist and folklorist who taught at Barnard College and Columbia University. She is best known for her work on the interconnectedness of personality, language, art, and culture, and for her text *Patterns of Culture*.

Sandra Ruth Lipsitz Bem (1944–2014) was an American psychologist. She is noted for her work in gender studies, particularly androgyny, gender roles, and gender polarization.

John W. Berry is a professor emeritus of psychology at Queen's University, Ontario. He is noted for his role in the development of the field of acculturation psychology.

Michael Harris Bond is a social psychologist at the Hong Kong Polytechnic University. He conducted the Chinese Value Survey and collaborated with Hofstede to define the fifth dimension of culture (long- versus short-term orientation).

Adriaan de Groot (1914–2006) was a Dutch psychologist and chess master who worked at the University of Amsterdam. He is best known for his studies of chess players, visual memory, and visual perception.

Edward T. Hall (1914–2009) was an American anthropologist who taught at many universities, among them Northwestern University in the United States. He is well known for his studies of intercultural communication and relations and his concept of social cohesion.

Michael H. Hoppe is an American senior program and research associate at the Center for Creative Leadership. He is known for his extensive work on cross-cultural leadership development and research.

Robert J. House was a professor at the Wharton School of the University of Pennsylvania. He is best known for organizing the GLOBE (Global Leadership and Organizational Behavior Effectiveness) world survey to examine national cultures.

Alex Inkeles (1920–2010) was an American sociologist who worked at the Hoover Institute and taught at Harvard University and Stanford University. He was a prolific scholar best known for his cross-national comparative studies and his work on an emerging worldwide society.

Çigdem Kagitçibasi is a Turkish psychologist at Koç University in Turkey. She is known for her work on educational, developmental, and health psychologies.

Clyde Kluckhohn (1905–60) was an American anthropologist at Harvard. He is best known for his ethnographic work on the Navajo Indians of the southwest United States and for developing the theory of culture.

Florence Kluckhohn was an American professor of sociology at Harvard. She co-authored *Variations in Value Orientations* with Fred Strodtbeck.

Daniel J. Levinson (1920–73) was an American psychologist working at Yale University. He is known for his theory of Stage-Crisis View, which used a holistic approach to understand the human life cycle.

Walter J. Lonner is a professor of psychology at Western Washington University. He is the author of *Psychology and Culture.*

Robert McCrae is a personality psychologist at the National Institute of Aging, Baltimore. He is well known for his Five Factor Theory of Personality.

Brendan McSweeney is a professor in the school of management at the University of London. His research explores financial economics, organizational studies, and human resources.

Margaret Mead (1901–78) was an American cultural anthropologist who worked at the American Museum of Natural History in New York. She was known for her cross-cultural work on gender and development explored in *Coming of Age in Samoa.* She helped to popularize anthropology through involvement with the media and general public.

Michael Minkov is a Bulgarian social anthropologist at the International University College in Bulgaria. His work examines cultural differences in society and management, and continues much of Hofstede's work through the expanded World Values Survey.

Marieke de Mooij is a Dutch emeritus professor of international advertisement at the University of Navarre in Spain. She is known for her research on the influence of culture on marketing and advertising.

Praveen Parboteeah is a professor of international management at the University of Wisconsin-Whitewater. His research examines cross-national differences in individual behavior.

Talcott Parsons (1902–79) was an American sociologist at Harvard. He is best known for his concept of "action theory" which studies society to balance positivist and idealist traditions. He co-authored *Toward a General Theory of Action* with Edward Shils.

Karl Popper (1902–17) was an influential Austrian-British philosopher of science. He is noted for his role in the development of modern scientific method, particularly the method of scientific inquiry generally known as empirical falsification.

Edward Shils (1910–95) was a Distinguished Service Professor of Sociology at the University of Chicago. He is known for his research on the role of intellectuals and their relationship to power and public policy. He co-authored *Toward a General Theory of Action* with Talcott Parsons.

Mikael Søndergaard is a Danish associate professor in the departments of management and economics at Aarhus University. In 1994, he conducted an analysis of 61 studies that replicated Hofstede's work and found that these independent results supported and verified Hofstede's findings about dimensions of culture.

Fred Strodtbeck (1919–2005) was a sociologist and psychologist at the University of Chicago. He is best known for his concept of microsociology, or how personalities interact in smaller groups. He co-authored the well-known text, *Variations in Value Orientations* with Florence Kluckhohn.

Harry Triandis (b. 1926) is a Greek American emeritus professor of psychology at the University of Illinois–Urbana-Champaign. He is known for examining the cognitive aspects of attitudes, norms, roles, and values across cultures.

WORKS CITED

WORKS CITED

Ailon, Galit. "Mirror, Mirror on the Wall: 'Culture's Consequences' in a Value Test of Its Own Design." *The Academy of Management Review*, no. 33 (2008): 885–904.

Bem, Sandra. "The Measurement of Psychological Androgyny." *Journal of Consulting and Clinical Psychology* 42 (1974): 155–162.

Benedict, Ruth. *Patterns of Culture*. Boston: Houghton Mifflin, 1959. (Originally published 1934).

Centre for Intercultural Learning. "Culture Does Not Exist." Accessed August 31, 2015, www.international.gc.ca/cil-cai/magazine/v02n03/1–3. aspx?lang=eng.

Chandy, P.R. and Thomas G. E. Williams. "The Impact of Journals and Authors on International Business Research: A Citational Analysis of *JIBS* Articles." *Journal of International Business Studies* 25 (1994): 715–728.

Goodrich, Kendall and Marieke de Mooij. "How 'social' are social media? A cross-cultural comparison of online and offline purchase decision influences." *Journal of Marketing Communications* 20 (2014): 103–116.

Hall, Edward T. *Beyond Culture*. Garden City, NY: Anchor, 1976.

Hart, William B. "Interdisciplinary influences in the study of intercultural relations: a citation analysis of the International Journal of Intercultural Relations." *International Journal of Intercultural Relations* 23 (1999): 575–589.

Hofstede, Geert. *Culture's Consequences: Comparing Values, Behaviors, Institutions, and Organizations across Nations*. Thousand Oaks, CA: Sage, 2001.

— "A reply and comment on Joginder P. Singh: "Managerial Culture and Work-Related Values in India," *Organization Studies*, 11 (1990): 103–106.

— *Cultures and Organizations: Software of the Mind*. New York: McGraw-Hill, 1991.

— "Dimensions Do Not Exist: A Reply to Brendan McSweeney." *Human Relations* 55 (2002): 1355–60.

— "What Did GLOBE Really Measure? Researchers' Minds Versus Respondents' Minds," *Journal of International Business Studies* 37 (2006): 882–896.

— "Who Is the Fairest of Them All? Galit Ailon's Mirror," *The Academy of*

Management Review 34 (2009): 570–571.

— "The Hofstede Centre." Accessed August 31, 2015, http://www.geerthofstede.com/geert.

Hoppe, Michael H. "A Comparative Study of Country Elites: International Differences in Work-Related Values and Learning and Their Implications for Management Training and Development." Unpublished PhD diss., University of North Carolina at Chapel Hill, 1990.

— "An Interview with Geert Hofstede," *The Academy of Management Executive (1993–2005)*, 18 (2004): 75–79.

House, Robert, Paul Hanges, Mansour Javidan, Peter Dorfman and Vipin Gupta. *Culture, Leadership, and Organizations: The GLOBE Study of 62 Societies*. Thousand Oaks, CA: Sage, 2004.

IBM Corporation. "Chronological History of IBM." Accessed September 4, 2015, http://www-03.ibm.com/ibm/history/history/history_intro.html

Inkeles, Alex and Daniel J. Levinson, "National Character: The Study of Modal Personality and Sociocultural Systems." In *Handbook of social psychology*, edited by Gardner Lindzey and Elliot Aronson, Vol. 4, 418-506. New York: McGraw-Hill, 1969. (Originally published 1954).

Javidan, Mansour, Robert House, Peter Dorfman, Paul Hanges and Mary Sully de Luque. "Conceptualizing and Measuring Cultures and their Consequences: A Comparative Review of GLOBE's and Hofstede's Approaches." *Journal of International Business Studies* 37 (2006): 897–914.

Jones, M. L. "Hofstede—Culturally questionable?," Paper presented at the Oxford Business & Economics Conference, Oxford, UK, June 24–26, 2007.

Kagitçibasi, Çigdem. "Social Norms and Authoritarianism: A Turkish-American Comparison." *Journal of Personality and Social Psychology* 16 (1970): 444–451.

Kluckhohn, Clyde. "Values and Value-Orientations in the Theory of Action: An Exploration in Definition and Classification." In *Toward a General Theory of Action*, edited by Talcott Parsons and Edward Shils, 388-433. Cambridge, MA: Harvard University Press, 1967. Original published in 1951.

Kluckhohn, Florence and Fred Strodtbeck. *Variations in Value Orientations*. Westport, CT: Greenwood, 1961.

Matusitz, Jonathan and George Musambira. "Power Distance, Uncertainty Avoidance, and Technology: Analyzing Hofstede's Dimensions and Human Development Indicators." *Journal of Technology in Human Services* 31 (2013): 42–60.

McSweeney, Brendan. "Hofstede's Model of National Cultural Differences and their Consequences: A Triumph of Faith—A Failure of Analysis." *Human Relations* 55 (2002): 89–118.

Mead, Margaret. *Coming of Age in Samoa: A Psychological Study of Primitive Youth for Western Civilization*. New York: Morrow, 1961.

Minkov, Michael. *Cultural Differences in a Globalizing World*. Bingley: Emerald, 2011.

de Mooij, Marieke. *Advertising Worldwide: Concepts, Theories and Practice of International, Multinational and Global Advertising*. Englewood Cliffs, NJ: Prentice Hall, 1994.

____. *Global Marketing and Advertising: Understanding Cultural Paradoxes*. Thousand Oaks, CA: Sage, 1998.

Parboteeah, Praveen and John Cullen. "Social Institutions and Work Centrality: Explorations beyond National Culture." *Organization Science* 14 (2003): 137–148.

Parsons, Talcott and Edward Shils. *Toward a General Theory of Action*. Cambridge, MA: Harvard University Press, 1951.

Shi, Xiumei and Jinying Wang. "Interpreting Hofstede Model and GLOBE Model: Which Way to Go for Cross-Cultural Research?" *International Journal of Business Management* 5 (2011): 93–99.

Smith, Peter B., Mark F. Peterson, and Shalom E. Schwartz, "Cultural Values, Sources of Guidance, and their Relevance to Managerial Behavior: A 47-nation study," *Journal of Cross-Cultural Psychology* 33, no. 22 (2002): 188–202.

Søndergaard, Mikael. "Research Note: Hofstede's Consequences: A Study of Reviews, Citations and Replications." *Organization Studies* 15 (1994): 447–456.

Taras, Vas, Julie Rowney, and Piers Steel. "Work-related acculturation: change in individual work-related cultural values following immigration." *The International Journal of Human Resource Management* 24 (2013): 130–151.

Triandis, Harry. "The Many Dimensions of Culture." *Academy of Management Executive* 18 (2004): 88-93.

Ybema, Sierk and Pál Nyíri. "The Hofstede Factor: the Consequences of *Culture's Consequences*." In *The Routledge Companion to Cross-Cultural Management*, edited by Nigel Holden, Snejina Michailova, and Susanne Tietze, 37–48. New York: Routledge, 2015.

THE MACAT LIBRARY
BY DISCIPLINE

AFRICANA STUDIES

Chinua Achebe's *An Image of Africa: Racism in Conrad's Heart of Darkness*
W. E. B. Du Bois's *The Souls of Black Folk*
Zora Neale Huston's *Characteristics of Negro Expression*
Martin Luther King Jr's *Why We Can't Wait*
Toni Morrison's *Playing in the Dark: Whiteness in the American Literary Imagination*

ANTHROPOLOGY

Arjun Appadurai's *Modernity at Large: Cultural Dimensions of Globalisation*
Philippe Ariès's *Centuries of Childhood*
Franz Boas's *Race, Language and Culture*
Kim Chan & Renée Mauborgne's *Blue Ocean Strategy*
Jared Diamond's *Guns, Germs & Steel: the Fate of Human Societies*
Jared Diamond's *Collapse: How Societies Choose to Fail or Survive*
E. E. Evans-Pritchard's *Witchcraft, Oracles and Magic Among the Azande*
James Ferguson's *The Anti-Politics Machine*
Clifford Geertz's *The Interpretation of Cultures*
David Graeber's *Debt: the First 5000 Years*
Karen Ho's *Liquidated: An Ethnography of Wall Street*
Geert Hofstede's *Culture's Consequences: Comparing Values, Behaviors, Institutes and Organizations across Nations*
Claude Lévi-Strauss's *Structural Anthropology*
Jay Macleod's *Ain't No Makin' It: Aspirations and Attainment in a Low-Income Neighborhood*
Saba Mahmood's *The Politics of Piety: The Islamic Revival and the Feminist Subject*
Marcel Mauss's *The Gift*

BUSINESS

Jean Lave & Etienne Wenger's *Situated Learning*
Theodore Levitt's *Marketing Myopia*
Burton G. Malkiel's *A Random Walk Down Wall Street*
Douglas McGregor's *The Human Side of Enterprise*
Michael Porter's *Competitive Strategy: Creating and Sustaining Superior Performance*
John Kotter's *Leading Change*
C. K. Prahalad & Gary Hamel's *The Core Competence of the Corporation*

CRIMINOLOGY

Michelle Alexander's *The New Jim Crow: Mass Incarceration in the Age of Colorblindness*
Michael R. Gottfredson & Travis Hirschi's *A General Theory of Crime*
Richard Herrnstein & Charles A. Murray's *The Bell Curve: Intelligence and Class Structure in American Life*
Elizabeth Loftus's *Eyewitness Testimony*
Jay Macleod's *Ain't No Makin' It: Aspirations and Attainment in a Low-Income Neighborhood*
Philip Zimbardo's *The Lucifer Effect*

ECONOMICS

Janet Abu-Lughod's *Before European Hegemony*
Ha-Joon Chang's *Kicking Away the Ladder*
David Brion Davis's *The Problem of Slavery in the Age of Revolution*
Milton Friedman's *The Role of Monetary Policy*
Milton Friedman's *Capitalism and Freedom*
David Graeber's *Debt: the First 5000 Years*
Friedrich Hayek's *The Road to Serfdom*
Karen Ho's *Liquidated: An Ethnography of Wall Street*

John Maynard Keynes's *The General Theory of Employment, Interest and Money*
Charles P. Kindleberger's *Manias, Panics and Crashes*
Robert Lucas's *Why Doesn't Capital Flow from Rich to Poor Countries?*
Burton G. Malkiel's *A Random Walk Down Wall Street*
Thomas Robert Malthus's *An Essay on the Principle of Population*
Karl Marx's *Capital*
Thomas Piketty's *Capital in the Twenty-First Century*
Amartya Sen's *Development as Freedom*
Adam Smith's *The Wealth of Nations*
Nassim Nicholas Taleb's *The Black Swan: The Impact of the Highly Improbable*
Amos Tversky's & Daniel Kahneman's *Judgment under Uncertainty: Heuristics and Biases*
Mahbub Ul Haq's *Reflections on Human Development*
Max Weber's *The Protestant Ethic and the Spirit of Capitalism*

FEMINISM AND GENDER STUDIES

Judith Butler's *Gender Trouble*
Simone De Beauvoir's *The Second Sex*
Michel Foucault's *History of Sexuality*
Betty Friedan's *The Feminine Mystique*
Saba Mahmood's *The Politics of Piety: The Islamic Revival and the Feminist Subject*
Joan Wallach Scott's *Gender and the Politics of History*
Mary Wollstonecraft's *A Vindication of the Rights of Woman*
Virginia Woolf's *A Room of One's Own*

GEOGRAPHY

The Brundtland Report's *Our Common Future*
Rachel Carson's *Silent Spring*
Charles Darwin's *On the Origin of Species*
James Ferguson's *The Anti-Politics Machine*
Jane Jacobs's *The Death and Life of Great American Cities*
James Lovelock's *Gaia: A New Look at Life on Earth*
Amartya Sen's *Development as Freedom*
Mathis Wackernagel & William Rees's *Our Ecological Footprint*

HISTORY

Janet Abu-Lughod's *Before European Hegemony*
Benedict Anderson's *Imagined Communities*
Bernard Bailyn's *The Ideological Origins of the American Revolution*
Hanna Batatu's *The Old Social Classes And The Revolutionary Movements Of Iraq*
Christopher Browning's *Ordinary Men: Reserve Police Batallion 101 and the Final Solution in Poland*
Edmund Burke's *Reflections on the Revolution in France*
William Cronon's *Nature's Metropolis: Chicago And The Great West*
Alfred W. Crosby's *The Columbian Exchange*
Hamid Dabashi's *Iran: A People Interrupted*
David Brion Davis's *The Problem of Slavery in the Age of Revolution*
Nathalie Zemon Davis's *The Return of Martin Guerre*
Jared Diamond's *Guns, Germs & Steel: the Fate of Human Societies*
Frank Dikotter's *Mao's Great Famine*
John W Dower's *War Without Mercy: Race And Power In The Pacific War*
W. E. B. Du Bois's *The Souls of Black Folk*
Richard J. Evans's *In Defence of History*
Lucien Febvre's *The Problem of Unbelief in the 16th Century*
Sheila Fitzpatrick's *Everyday Stalinism*

The Macat Library By Discipline

Eric Foner's *Reconstruction: America's Unfinished Revolution, 1863-1877*
Michel Foucault's *Discipline and Punish*
Michel Foucault's *History of Sexuality*
Francis Fukuyama's *The End of History and the Last Man*
John Lewis Gaddis's *We Now Know: Rethinking Cold War History*
Ernest Gellner's *Nations and Nationalism*
Eugene Genovese's *Roll, Jordan, Roll: The World the Slaves Made*
Carlo Ginzburg's *The Night Battles*
Daniel Goldhagen's *Hitler's Willing Executioners*
Jack Goldstone's *Revolution and Rebellion in the Early Modern World*
Antonio Gramsci's *The Prison Notebooks*
Alexander Hamilton, John Jay & James Madison's *The Federalist Papers*
Christopher Hill's *The World Turned Upside Down*
Carole Hillenbrand's *The Crusades: Islamic Perspectives*
Thomas Hobbes's *Leviathan*
Eric Hobsbawm's *The Age Of Revolution*
John A. Hobson's *Imperialism: A Study*
Albert Hourani's *History of the Arab Peoples*
Samuel P. Huntington's *The Clash of Civilizations and the Remaking of World Order*
C. L. R. James's *The Black Jacobins*
Tony Judt's *Postwar: A History of Europe Since 1945*
Ernst Kantorowicz's *The King's Two Bodies: A Study in Medieval Political Theology*
Paul Kennedy's *The Rise and Fall of the Great Powers*
Ian Kershaw's *The "Hitler Myth": Image and Reality in the Third Reich*
John Maynard Keynes's *The General Theory of Employment, Interest and Money*
Charles P. Kindleberger's *Manias, Panics and Crashes*
Martin Luther King Jr's *Why We Can't Wait*
Henry Kissinger's *World Order: Reflections on the Character of Nations and the Course of History*
Thomas Kuhn's *The Structure of Scientific Revolutions*
Georges Lefebvre's *The Coming of the French Revolution*
John Locke's *Two Treatises of Government*
Niccolò Machiavelli's *The Prince*
Thomas Robert Malthus's *An Essay on the Principle of Population*
Mahmood Mamdani's *Citizen and Subject: Contemporary Africa And The Legacy Of Late Colonialism*
Karl Marx's *Capital*
Stanley Milgram's *Obedience to Authority*
John Stuart Mill's *On Liberty*
Thomas Paine's *Common Sense*
Thomas Paine's *Rights of Man*
Geoffrey Parker's *Global Crisis: War, Climate Change and Catastrophe in the Seventeenth Century*
Jonathan Riley-Smith's *The First Crusade and the Idea of Crusading*
Jean-Jacques Rousseau's *The Social Contract*
Joan Wallach Scott's *Gender and the Politics of History*
Theda Skocpol's *States and Social Revolutions*
Adam Smith's *The Wealth of Nations*
Timothy Snyder's *Bloodlands: Europe Between Hitler and Stalin*
Sun Tzu's *The Art of War*
Keith Thomas's *Religion and the Decline of Magic*
Thucydides's *The History of the Peloponnesian War*
Frederick Jackson Turner's *The Significance of the Frontier in American History*
Odd Arne Westad's *The Global Cold War: Third World Interventions And The Making Of Our Times*

The Macat Library By Discipline

LITERATURE

Chinua Achebe's *An Image of Africa: Racism in Conrad's Heart of Darkness*
Roland Barthes's *Mythologies*
Homi K. Bhabha's *The Location of Culture*
Judith Butler's *Gender Trouble*
Simone De Beauvoir's *The Second Sex*
Ferdinand De Saussure's *Course in General Linguistics*
T. S. Eliot's *The Sacred Wood: Essays on Poetry and Criticism*
Zora Neale Huston's *Characteristics of Negro Expression*
Toni Morrison's *Playing in the Dark: Whiteness in the American Literary Imagination*
Edward Said's *Orientalism*
Gayatri Chakravorty Spivak's *Can the Subaltern Speak?*
Mary Wollstonecraft's *A Vindication of the Rights of Women*
Virginia Woolf's *A Room of One's Own*

PHILOSOPHY

Elizabeth Anscombe's *Modern Moral Philosophy*
Hannah Arendt's *The Human Condition*
Aristotle's *Metaphysics*
Aristotle's *Nicomachean Ethics*
Edmund Gettier's *Is Justified True Belief Knowledge?*
Georg Wilhelm Friedrich Hegel's *Phenomenology of Spirit*
David Hume's *Dialogues Concerning Natural Religion*
David Hume's *The Enquiry for Human Understanding*
Immanuel Kant's *Religion within the Boundaries of Mere Reason*
Immanuel Kant's *Critique of Pure Reason*
Søren Kierkegaard's *The Sickness Unto Death*
Søren Kierkegaard's *Fear and Trembling*
C. S. Lewis's *The Abolition of Man*
Alasdair MacIntyre's *After Virtue*
Marcus Aurelius's *Meditations*
Friedrich Nietzsche's *On the Genealogy of Morality*
Friedrich Nietzsche's *Beyond Good and Evil*
Plato's *Republic*
Plato's *Symposium*
Jean-Jacques Rousseau's *The Social Contract*
Gilbert Ryle's *The Concept of Mind*
Baruch Spinoza's *Ethics*
Sun Tzu's *The Art of War*
Ludwig Wittgenstein's *Philosophical Investigations*

POLITICS

Benedict Anderson's *Imagined Communities*
Aristotle's *Politics*
Bernard Bailyn's *The Ideological Origins of the American Revolution*
Edmund Burke's *Reflections on the Revolution in France*
John C. Calhoun's *A Disquisition on Government*
Ha-Joon Chang's *Kicking Away the Ladder*
Hamid Dabashi's *Iran: A People Interrupted*
Hamid Dabashi's *Theology of Discontent: The Ideological Foundation of the Islamic Revolution in Iran*
Robert Dahl's *Democracy and its Critics*
Robert Dahl's *Who Governs?*
David Brion Davis's *The Problem of Slavery in the Age of Revolution*

Alexis De Tocqueville's *Democracy in America*
James Ferguson's *The Anti-Politics Machine*
Frank Dikotter's *Mao's Great Famine*
Sheila Fitzpatrick's *Everyday Stalinism*
Eric Foner's *Reconstruction: America's Unfinished Revolution, 1863-1877*
Milton Friedman's *Capitalism and Freedom*
Francis Fukuyama's *The End of History and the Last Man*
John Lewis Gaddis's *We Now Know: Rethinking Cold War History*
Ernest Gellner's *Nations and Nationalism*
David Graeber's *Debt: the First 5000 Years*
Antonio Gramsci's *The Prison Notebooks*
Alexander Hamilton, John Jay & James Madison's *The Federalist Papers*
Friedrich Hayek's *The Road to Serfdom*
Christopher Hill's *The World Turned Upside Down*
Thomas Hobbes's *Leviathan*
John A. Hobson's *Imperialism: A Study*
Samuel P. Huntington's *The Clash of Civilizations and the Remaking of World Order*
Tony Judt's *Postwar: A History of Europe Since 1945*
David C. Kang's *China Rising: Peace, Power and Order in East Asia*
Paul Kennedy's *The Rise and Fall of Great Powers*
Robert Keohane's *After Hegemony*
Martin Luther King Jr.'s *Why We Can't Wait*
Henry Kissinger's *World Order: Reflections on the Character of Nations and the Course of History*
John Locke's *Two Treatises of Government*
Niccolò Machiavelli's *The Prince*
Thomas Robert Malthus's *An Essay on the Principle of Population*
Mahmood Mamdani's *Citizen and Subject: Contemporary Africa And The Legacy Of Late Colonialism*
Karl Marx's *Capital*
John Stuart Mill's *On Liberty*
John Stuart Mill's *Utilitarianism*
Hans Morgenthau's *Politics Among Nations*
Thomas Paine's *Common Sense*
Thomas Paine's *Rights of Man*
Thomas Piketty's *Capital in the Twenty-First Century*
Robert D. Putman's *Bowling Alone*
John Rawls's *Theory of Justice*
Jean-Jacques Rousseau's *The Social Contract*
Theda Skocpol's *States and Social Revolutions*
Adam Smith's *The Wealth of Nations*
Sun Tzu's *The Art of War*
Henry David Thoreau's *Civil Disobedience*
Thucydides's *The History of the Peloponnesian War*
Kenneth Waltz's *Theory of International Politics*
Max Weber's *Politics as a Vocation*
Odd Arne Westad's *The Global Cold War: Third World Interventions And The Making Of Our Times*

POSTCOLONIAL STUDIES

Roland Barthes's *Mythologies*
Frantz Fanon's *Black Skin, White Masks*
Homi K. Bhabha's *The Location of Culture*
Gustavo Gutiérrez's *A Theology of Liberation*
Edward Said's *Orientalism*
Gayatri Chakravorty Spivak's *Can the Subaltern Speak?*

PSYCHOLOGY

Gordon Allport's *The Nature of Prejudice*
Alan Baddeley & Graham Hitch's *Aggression: A Social Learning Analysis*
Albert Bandura's *Aggression: A Social Learning Analysis*
Leon Festinger's *A Theory of Cognitive Dissonance*
Sigmund Freud's *The Interpretation of Dreams*
Betty Friedan's *The Feminine Mystique*
Michael R. Gottfredson & Travis Hirschi's *A General Theory of Crime*
Eric Hoffer's *The True Believer: Thoughts on the Nature of Mass Movements*
William James's *Principles of Psychology*
Elizabeth Loftus's *Eyewitness Testimony*
A. H. Maslow's *A Theory of Human Motivation*
Stanley Milgram's *Obedience to Authority*
Steven Pinker's *The Better Angels of Our Nature*
Oliver Sacks's *The Man Who Mistook His Wife For a Hat*
Richard Thaler & Cass Sunstein's *Nudge: Improving Decisions About Health, Wealth and Happiness*
Amos Tversky's *Judgment under Uncertainty: Heuristics and Biases*
Philip Zimbardo's *The Lucifer Effect*

SCIENCE

Rachel Carson's *Silent Spring*
William Cronon's *Nature's Metropolis: Chicago And The Great West*
Alfred W. Crosby's *The Columbian Exchange*
Charles Darwin's *On the Origin of Species*
Richard Dawkin's *The Selfish Gene*
Thomas Kuhn's *The Structure of Scientific Revolutions*
Geoffrey Parker's *Global Crisis: War, Climate Change and Catastrophe in the Seventeenth Century*
Mathis Wackernagel & William Rees's *Our Ecological Footprint*

SOCIOLOGY

Michelle Alexander's *The New Jim Crow: Mass Incarceration in the Age of Colorblindness*
Gordon Allport's *The Nature of Prejudice*
Albert Bandura's *Aggression: A Social Learning Analysis*
Hanna Batatu's *The Old Social Classes And The Revolutionary Movements Of Iraq*
Ha-Joon Chang's *Kicking Away the Ladder*
W. E. B. Du Bois's *The Souls of Black Folk*
Émile Durkheim's *On Suicide*
Frantz Fanon's *Black Skin, White Masks*
Frantz Fanon's *The Wretched of the Earth*
Eric Foner's *Reconstruction: America's Unfinished Revolution, 1863-1877*
Eugene Genovese's *Roll, Jordan, Roll: The World the Slaves Made*
Jack Goldstone's *Revolution and Rebellion in the Early Modern World*
Antonio Gramsci's *The Prison Notebooks*
Richard Herrnstein & Charles A Murray's *The Bell Curve: Intelligence and Class Structure in American Life*
Eric Hoffer's *The True Believer: Thoughts on the Nature of Mass Movements*
Jane Jacobs's *The Death and Life of Great American Cities*
Robert Lucas's *Why Doesn't Capital Flow from Rich to Poor Countries?*
Jay Macleod's *Ain't No Makin' It: Aspirations and Attainment in a Low Income Neighborhood*
Elaine May's *Homeward Bound: American Families in the Cold War Era*
Douglas McGregor's *The Human Side of Enterprise*
C. Wright Mills's *The Sociological Imagination*

Thomas Piketty's *Capital in the Twenty-First Century*
Robert D. Putman's *Bowling Alone*
David Riesman's *The Lonely Crowd: A Study of the Changing American Character*
Edward Said's *Orientalism*
Joan Wallach Scott's *Gender and the Politics of History*
Theda Skocpol's *States and Social Revolutions*
Max Weber's *The Protestant Ethic and the Spirit of Capitalism*

THEOLOGY

Augustine's *Confessions*
Benedict's *Rule of St Benedict*
Gustavo Gutiérrez's *A Theology of Liberation*
Carole Hillenbrand's *The Crusades: Islamic Perspectives*
David Hume's *Dialogues Concerning Natural Religion*
Immanuel Kant's *Religion within the Boundaries of Mere Reason*
Ernst Kantorowicz's *The King's Two Bodies: A Study in Medieval Political Theology*
Søren Kierkegaard's *The Sickness Unto Death*
C. S. Lewis's *The Abolition of Man*
Saba Mahmood's *The Politics of Piety: The Islamic Revival and the Feminist Subject*
Baruch Spinoza's *Ethics*
Keith Thomas's *Religion and the Decline of Magic*

COMING SOON

Chris Argyris's *The Individual and the Organisation*
Seyla Benhabib's *The Rights of Others*
Walter Benjamin's *The Work Of Art in the Age of Mechanical Reproduction*
John Berger's *Ways of Seeing*
Pierre Bourdieu's *Outline of a Theory of Practice*
Mary Douglas's *Purity and Danger*
Roland Dworkin's *Taking Rights Seriously*
James G. March's *Exploration and Exploitation in Organisational Learning*
Ikujiro Nonaka's *A Dynamic Theory of Organizational Knowledge Creation*
Griselda Pollock's *Vision and Difference*
Amartya Sen's *Inequality Re-Examined*
Susan Sontag's *On Photography*
Yasser Tabbaa's *The Transformation of Islamic Art*
Ludwig von Mises's *Theory of Money and Credit*

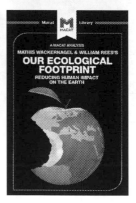

Macat Disciplines

Access the greatest ideas and thinkers across entire disciplines, including

INEQUALITY

Ha-Joon Chang's, *Kicking Away the Ladder*

David Graeber's, *Debt: The First 5000 Years*

Robert E. Lucas's, *Why Doesn't Capital Flow from Rich To Poor Countries?*

Thomas Piketty's, *Capital in the Twenty-First Century*

Amartya Sen's, *Inequality Re-Examined*

Mahbub Ul Haq's, *Reflections on Human Development*

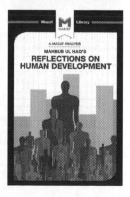

Macat analyses are available from all good bookshops and libraries.

Access hundreds of analyses through one, multimedia tool.
Join free for one month **library.macat.com**

Macat Disciplines

Access the greatest ideas and thinkers across entire disciplines, including

THE FUTURE OF DEMOCRACY

Robert A. Dahl's, *Democracy and Its Critics*
Robert A. Dahl's, *Who Governs?*
Alexis De Toqueville's, *Democracy in America*
Niccolò Machiavelli's, *The Prince*
John Stuart Mill's, *On Liberty*
Robert D. Putnam's, *Bowling Alone*
Jean-Jacques Rousseau's, *The Social Contract*
Henry David Thoreau's, *Civil Disobedience*

Macat Disciplines

Access the greatest ideas and thinkers across entire disciplines, including

Postcolonial Studies

Roland Barthes's *Mythologies*
Frantz Fanon's *Black Skin, White Masks*
Homi K. Bhabha's *The Location of Culture*
Gustavo Gutiérrez's *A Theology of Liberation*
Edward Said's *Orientalism*
Gayatri Chakravorty Spivak's *Can the Subaltern Speak?*

Macat analyses are available from all good bookshops and libraries.

Access hundreds of analyses through one, multimedia tool.

Macat Disciplines

*Access the greatest ideas and thinkers
across entire disciplines, including*

AFRICANA STUDIES

Chinua Achebe's *An Image of Africa:
Racism in Conrad's Heart of Darkness*

W. E. B. Du Bois's *The Souls of Black Folk*

Zora Neale Hurston's *Characteristics of Negro Expression*

Martin Luther King Jr.'s *Why We Can't Wait*

Toni Morrison's *Playing in the Dark:
Whiteness in the American Literary Imagination*

Macat analyses are available from all good bookshops and libraries.

Access hundreds of analyses through one, multimedia tool.

Macat Disciplines

Access the greatest ideas and thinkers across entire disciplines, including

FEMINISM, GENDER AND QUEER STUDIES

Simone De Beauvoir's
The Second Sex

Michel Foucault's
History of Sexuality

Betty Friedan's
The Feminine Mystique

Saba Mahmood's
*The Politics of Piety:
The Islamic Revival and
the Feminist Subject*

Joan Wallach Scott's
*Gender and the
Politics of History*

Mary Wollstonecraft's
*A Vindication of the
Rights of Woman*

Virginia Woolf's
A Room of One's Own

Judith Butler's
Gender Trouble

Macat analyses are available from all good bookshops and libraries.

Access hundreds of analyses through one, multimedia tool.
Join free for one month **library.macat.com**

Macat Disciplines

Access the greatest ideas and thinkers across entire disciplines, including

CRIMINOLOGY

Michelle Alexander's
*The New Jim Crow:
Mass Incarceration in the
Age of Colorblindness*

**Michael R. Gottfredson
& Travis Hirschi's**
A General Theory of Crime

Elizabeth Loftus's
Eyewitness Testimony

**Richard Herrnstein
& Charles A. Murray's**
*The Bell Curve: Intelligence and
Class Structure in American Life*

Jay Macleod's
*Ain't No Makin' It:
Aspirations and Attainment in a
Low-Income Neighborhood*

Philip Zimbardo's
The Lucifer Effect

Macat analyses are available from all good bookshops and libraries.

Access hundreds of analyses through one, multimedia tool.

Macat Disciplines

Access the greatest ideas and thinkers across entire disciplines, including

GLOBALIZATION

Arjun Appadurai's, *Modernity at Large: Cultural Dimensions of Globalisation*

James Ferguson's, *The Anti-Politics Machine*

Geert Hofstede's, *Culture's Consequences*

Amartya Sen's, *Development as Freedom*

Macat analyses are available from all good bookshops and libraries.

Access hundreds of analyses through one, multimedia tool.

Join free for one month **library.macat.com**

Macat Disciplines

Access the greatest ideas and thinkers across entire disciplines, including

TOTALITARIANISM

Sheila Fitzpatrick's, *Everyday Stalinism*
Ian Kershaw's, *The "Hitler Myth"*
Timothy Snyder's, *Bloodlands*

Macat analyses are available from all good bookshops and libraries.

Access hundreds of analyses through one, multimedia tool.

Join free for one month **library.macat.com**

Macat Pairs

*Analyse historical and modern issues
from opposite sides of an argument.
Pairs include:*

RACE AND IDENTITY

Zora Neale Hurston's
Characteristics of Negro Expression

Using material collected on anthropological expeditions to the South, Zora Neale Hurston explains how expression in African American culture in the early twentieth century departs from the art of white America. At the time, African American art was often criticized for copying white culture. For Hurston, this criticism misunderstood how art works. European tradition views art as something fixed. But Hurston describes a creative process that is alive, ever-changing, and largely improvisational. She maintains that African American art works through a process called 'mimicry'—where an imitated object or verbal pattern, for example, is reshaped and altered until it becomes something new, novel—and worthy of attention.

Frantz Fanon's
Black Skin, White Masks

Black Skin, White Masks offers a radical analysis of the psychological effects of colonization on the colonized.

Fanon witnessed the effects of colonization first hand both in his birthplace, Martinique, and again later in life when he worked as a psychiatrist in another French colony, Algeria. His text is uncompromising in form and argument. He dissects the dehumanizing effects of colonialism, arguing that it destroys the native sense of identity, forcing people to adapt to an alien set of values—including a core belief that they are inferior. This results in deep psychological trauma.

Fanon's work played a pivotal role in the civil rights movements of the 1960s.

Macat analyses are available from all good bookshops and libraries.

Access hundreds of analyses through one, multimedia tool.
Join free for one month **library.macat.com**

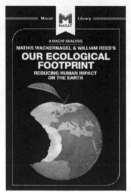

Printed in the United States
by Baker & Taylor Publisher Services